HOLY BAPTISM
AND
SERVICES FOR THE RENEWAL
OF BAPTISM

HOLY BAPTISM
AND
SERVICES FOR THE RENEWAL OF BAPTISM

The Worship of God

Supplemental Liturgical Resource 2

Prepared by

The Office of Worship
for the
Presbyterian Church (U.S.A.)
and the
Cumberland Presbyterian Church

Published by
The Westminster Press
Philadelphia

Published by The Westminster Press®
Philadelphia, Pennsylvania

PRINTED IN THE UNITED STATES OF AMERICA
4   6   8   9   7   5

Library of Congress Cataloging in Publication Data

Presbyterian Church (U.S.A.)
    Holy baptism ; and, Services for the renewal of baptism.

    (Supplemental liturgical resource ; 2)
    Bibliography: p.
    1. Baptism—Presbyterian Church (U.S.A.)—Liturgy—Texts. 2. Baptism—Cumberland Presbyterian Church—Liturgy—Texts. 3. Baptism—Presbyterian Church—Liturgy—Texts. 4. Baptism—Reaffirmation of covenant—Presbyterian Church (U.S.A.)—Liturgy—Texts. 5. Baptism—Reaffirmation of covenant—Cumberland Presbyterian Church—Liturgy—Texts. 6. Baptism—Reaffirmation of covenant—Presbyterian Church—Liturgy—Texts. 7. Presbyterian Church (U.S.A.)—Liturgy—Texts. 8. Cumberland Presbyterian Church—Liturgy—Texts. 9. Presbyterian Church—Liturgy—Texts. I. Office of Worship (U.S.) II. Cumberland Presbyterian Church. III. Presbyterian Church (U.S.A.). Renewal of baptism. © 1985. IV. Title: Holy baptism. V. Title: Services for the renewal of baptism. VI. Series: Presbyterian Church (U.S.A.). Supplemental liturgical resource ; 2.
BX8969.5.P74 1985   264'.05137   85-3137
ISBN 0-664-24647-8 (pbk.)

CONTENTS

PREFACE

In 1980, the antecedent denominations of the Presbyterian Church (U.S.A.) took action to begin the process to develop "a new book of services for corporate worship, including a Psalter, hymns, and other worship aids." The churches asked that over the "next several years a variety of worship resources be made available . . . for trial use throughout the church before any publication is finalized." In this action the church expressed a hope that such a book and the process leading to it "would provide a new instrument for the renewal of the church at its life-giving center." Subsequent action by the Cumberland Presbyterian Church made it a partner in the project.

Holy Baptism and Services for the Renewal of Baptism is the second volume in the series of trial-use liturgical resources that is resulting from the General Assembly actions. Other resources being developed include daily prayer, the psalms, Christian marriage, Christian burial, the Christian year, ordination, ministry to the sick and the dying, the lectionary, and service music. When the series of resources is completed, the material that will have appeared will be further revised and combined in a new book of services.

In developing the resources, guidance on worship policy is given by the Advisory Council on Discipleship and Worship through its Committee on Worship.

A task force of persons with expertise in the particular subject of the resource to be developed is appointed by the Administrative Committee of the Office of Worship to prepare a manuscript on an assigned portion of the church's liturgy. In the fall of 1980, a task force was appointed to prepare a resource for the celebration of baptism and for rites related to baptism. *Holy Baptism and Services for the Renewal of Baptism* is the result of the work of that task force.

General Assembly actions in 1981 were to affect further the work of this task force when the General Assembly approved recommendations to write a new Directory for Worship. In response to a number of overtures received by the General Assembly concerning the nature of baptism and its relationship to the Lord's Supper, the Advisory Council on Discipleship and Worship and the Council on Theology and Culture established a joint task force to write a new chapter on baptism for the Directory for Worship. In light of this decision, the schedule of the task force preparing this resource was lengthened so that work on the Directory chapter on baptism could inform the developing of the new baptismal rite. During their life spans, the two task forces worked in close relationship with each other. Each task force reviewed and commented on the other's work and on occasion met together in joint session.

As a result, this order for baptism is firmly based upon the proposed chapter on baptism prepared for the new Directory for Worship, which was received for study by the 196th General Assembly (1984) of the Presbyterian Church (U.S.A.).

Those who served on the task force that prepared *Holy Baptism and Services for the Renewal of Baptism* were Robert M. Shelton, chairperson; Catherine Gunsalus González; Roger A. Martin; V. Bruce Rigdon; and Harold M. Daniels, staff.

Those who served on the task force preparing the "Proposed Chapter on Baptism for a New Directory for Worship" were Donald R. Purkey, chairperson; Melva W. Costen; Arlo D. Duba; Joan S. Gray; John F. Jansen; V. Bruce Rigdon; Joan SalmonCampbell; Byron E. Shafer; Margaret Veneman; John Ed Withers; James G. Kirk, staff; and Harold M. Daniels, resource consultant.

Each manuscript that is developed in the Supplemental Liturgical Resource series is carefully reviewed by the Worship Committee of the Advisory Council on Discipleship and Worship, which makes suggestions for its revision. Members of the Worship Committee reviewing *Holy Baptism and Services for the Renewal of Baptism* were Donald W. Stake, chairperson; Moffet Swaim Churn; Melva W. Costen; Craig D. Erickson; Frances M. Gray; Robert S. Moorhead; Franklin E. Perkins; J. Barrie Shepherd; Helen Wright; James G. Kirk, staff; Elizabeth J. Villegas, staff; and Harold M. Daniels, adjunct staff.

Holy Baptism and Services for the Renewal of Baptism was extensively field-tested. Suggestions were also sought from liturgical scholars both in the Reformed tradition and in other traditions. The evaluations and suggestions that were received contributed greatly to the improvement of this resource, and we are therefore indebted to many people for their invaluable assistance.

Responding to the field-testing and review, the task force prepared the final draft of this resource and presented it to the Administrative Committee of the Office of Worship. The Administrative Committee, which had overseen the work of the task force during the years the resource was being developed, then approved the manuscript for publication. Those who served on the Administrative Committee during the time *Holy Baptism and Services for the Renewal of Baptism* was being developed were Melva W. Costen; Arlo D. Duba; Lucile L. Hair (former chairperson); Collier S. Harvey; James G. Kirk; Wynn McGregor; Ray Meester; Robert D. Miller; Clementine Morrison; Betty Peek; David C. Partington (current chairperson); Dorothea Snyder (former chairperson); Robert Stigall; Darius L. Swann; James Vande Berg; Harold M. Daniels, staff; and Marion L. Liebert, staff.

We invite your evaluation of this resource presented to the church for trial use as it anticipates a new book of services. Send your comments to the Office of Worship, 1044 Alta Vista Road, Louisville, Kentucky 40205.

We commend this volume for your use. May it assist the church to discover a new appreciation for this sacrament that is central to the church and the Christian life.

HAROLD M. DANIELS, Director
Office of Worship

HOLY BAPTISM

BAPTISM: PROBLEMS AND PROMISE

Recently the members of a high school youth fellowship group in a local congregation were asked, "What does your baptism mean to you?" Without exception all of them answered, "Nothing." When their reasons for this response were sought, they replied that it was because none of them could remember his or her baptism. On further reflection they confessed that they were not sure that they understood what baptism was all about and that the church had never made this very clear to them.

In a Presbyterian congregation in a small town, Mrs. Jones, an elder for nearly twenty years, approaches her pastor to ask whether or not next Sunday would be a good time to baptize her grandson who will be visiting for the weekend. Her daughter and son-in-law live in a city several hundred miles away and have not attended church since they were married. Mrs. Jones is eager to have the baptism take place at a time when as many family members as possible can be present. She will be deeply hurt if the pastor does not agree to "do the ceremony."

A fourteen-year-old girl is asked by her parents to enroll in the confirmation class offered at her church. She is told by her parents that the class will prepare her "to join the church." She answers with some surprise, "I thought that I joined the church when I was baptized." Her parents do not know how to respond.

"Is one expected to demonstrate a different manner of living because of baptism?" asked a sixteen-year-old black male. "Is racism accepted behavior? Maybe baptism doesn't make a difference . . . it's just another empty ritual." His cabin director at the presbytery camp, opened for the first time to racial and ethnic minorities, sat and stared at him.

A woman who was brought up in the Presbyterian Church marries a man who is a member of an independent Baptist church. When she seeks to join her husband's church, she is told by the pastor that she must be baptized again, since infant baptism is not a "baptism of repentance."

These five vignettes illustrate something of the extraordinary confusion about baptism in the church today. This confusion is so deep and so extensive that it has taken on the proportion of a crisis. It is not, as some might suppose, simply a question of what rites and practices are appropriate. Rather, it has to do with the very roots of what the church believes and confesses about God's grace, the nature of faith, and the meaning of Christian community. In short, it has to do with the most fundamental elements of Christian faith and life.

These vignettes have been reenacted many times in our country and abroad. They reveal different aspects of the crisis and point to basic questions with respect to baptism: What does baptism mean? Who is to be baptized? What is the relationship of baptism to church membership? What is the relationship of baptism to repentance and personal faith?

The Meaning of Baptism

Many church members do not understand what baptism means. The prevailing confusion in teaching and practice makes such an understanding difficult to achieve. This is partly a result of the church's failure to provide adequate theological and liturgical education about the sacraments. Despite the abundance of recent research and writing on baptism, for example, few materials are available for Presbyterian parents and children, for the laity of our congregations, concerning baptismal issues. The problem, however, cannot be entirely resolved by our publishing houses.

Worshipers witness baptisms with some regularity. In Presbyterian churches most of these are baptisms of infants and young children. Baptism is considered a happy moment. Congregations are amused and intrigued by the various responses of babies. But there is little sense that the child is undergoing a profound initiation, a process of cleansing from sin, of entering into the death and resurrection of Christ, and of being received into a new community or family of faith. Few would understand what is happening as a life-changing and transforming event, one with fundamental repercussions for the rest of the child's life. Instead, the congregation hears some words spoken, sees a little water sprinkled, makes some formal promises to nurture the child in faith—and the whole event is over in a matter of minutes. Nothing important appears to be changed as a result of this ceremony. Even the date when the event occurred, though preserved in church records, is soon forgotten by both the congregation and the baptized. Life goes on as usual. The child may be assimilated into the congregation or may disappear; he or she may be found in later years in the choir, the church youth group or scout troop, or the confirmation class, but it is not really clear whether or not these involvements have anything to do with water and baptism.

If baptism is to communicate the powerful meanings which it has embodied for Christians throughout our history, the rite or ceremony itself must be experienced as an event of great importance; it must in fact be the beginning of a process for which the whole congregation takes responsibility. But one of the greatest difficulties in understanding the meaning of baptism is that the Christian believer is cut off from the very events and realities to which baptism refers.

The origins of this sacrament are to be found in ancient liturgical washings, the baptism of Jesus by John and the death and resurrection of our Lord Jesus Christ. Most North American Christians have never experienced drought or flood and do not view water either as a valuable commodity or as having the potential for spiritual potency. A significant exception is the experience of Native Americans and Blacks. Water has been a powerful spiritual symbol both in Native American traditions and in the African heritage of Black Americans. Black Americans have entered into the experiences of crossing the Jordan to the Promised Land ("Deep river, I want to cross over into campground"), deliverance after wandering in the wilderness ("Tell me, how did you feel when you come out the wilderness?") and standing on Golgotha at the foot of the cross ("Were you there, when they crucified my Lord?"). These are the fundamental experiences which baptism recalls and to which its rich symbols point. By approximating the experience of Native Americans, Blacks, and other racial and ethnic minorities, all Presbyterians will be helped to claim those experiences which baptism recalls. One who is baptized must also be willing to appropriate the faith journeys of particular members of Christ's body as the legitimate inheritance of all.

The renewal of the experience of baptism depends, as always, upon powerful preaching and teaching, upon the wise use of the

sacrament's signs and symbols, and upon taking with real serious-
ness the responsibilities which grow out of baptism as a gift of grace.
Baptism itself is one of the experiences of the biblical witness that
God has chosen to be gracious, and that this grace comes to us in
and through the natural elements of the world which God has
created.

The Recipients of Baptism

Baptism inevitably poses questions as to who should receive it and
under what conditions it should be administered. These are very old
questions in the history of the church. Ever since the legitimation of
the Christian religion by the Emperor Constantine in the fourth century, Christianity has had a close identification with culture. By the
end of that century, with the exception of the Jews, to be a citizen of
the Roman Empire was by law to be a Christian. With some notable
exceptions, close connections between church and state were to
characterize Christianity in both East and West until relatively recent
times.

For the church in the West, this led to the practice of establishing
state churches, whether Roman Catholic or Protestant. Even today,
many such state churches exist in Western Europe, financed by public
monies and regulated by public policies. This has led to "church
registration," in which a child is born, registered, and baptized without regard to whether or not the parents are active participants in a
local congregation. Indeed, unless legal action is taken to dissolve
this church connection, the child will pay a tax for church support
throughout his or her life. Thus birth, baptism, and citizenship are
inextricably bound together.

Events in Europe leading to World War II brought this phenomenon to an unprecedented crisis. Some major theologians challenged
ancient practice when they asserted that it was blasphemous to baptize children who would grow up to don jackboots and participate in
the persecution of Jews and other non-Aryans. No less eminent a
theologian than Karl Barth urged the church to give up the baptism
of infants and to place before mature persons the radical decision as
to whether or not they chose to live as Christians in a society that
could no longer be understood to be Christian. Though Emil Brunner
and other prominent Reformed theologians disagreed with Barth's
conclusion, they were no less convinced than he that society could
no longer be equated with Christianity.

Brunner refused to give up baptism of infants because it was such a vivid testimony to the conviction that it is God who acts graciously toward us in baptism and that this grace is not earned but freely given; not even our decision merits this divine goodness. Brunner argued that the church should not reject the baptism of infants but seek to reclaim it, by taking most seriously its responsibilities to see that those baptized would be nurtured in faith through participation in the church's life and ministry. Only if such conditions could be secured could an infant be baptized into the church.

In the United States, with its historic constitutional separation of church and state, we have not experienced the phenomenon of "registration." Nonetheless, we have inherited some of the attitudes prevalent in Western Europe. For large numbers in our churches, and in society, baptism has come to be viewed as a cultural practice. The association of Christianity with culture in our context is reflected in a phenomenon called American civil religion, which equates God and country as entities demanding the same loyalties and having the same intentions or goals. But baptism is not an initiation into citizenship or the American way of life; rather, it is initiation into the church, where ultimate loyalty belongs to Christ alone and where life must be shaped by the demands of the gospel. Being a Christian is not a function of being a good American. Rather, being a good citizen of this or any other country is a function of being loyal to Christ.

If the church takes this seriously, the renewal of baptism requires that everyone—parents or guardians, the session, and the whole congregation—must see that baptism is administered only to those who will be responsibly nurtured through participation in the worship and work of the church. To do less than this is to empty the sacrament of its meaning and to hide the graciousness of God from those who seek it.

Baptism and Church Membership

Baptism's relation to confirmation (and to the Lord's Supper) continues to be a source of great confusion. Early in the church's history in both East and West, baptism, confirmation, and Holy Communion were administered together as a celebration of the entrance of new Christians, whether infants or adults, into the church. For a time this celebration typically occurred during the night before Easter, when the congregation gathered to celebrate the resurrection of Christ. Easter was originally a baptismal feast, thus establishing the closest connection between baptism itself and Christ's own death and resurrection.

New Christians were baptized, usually just outside the church (in baptisteries) or at the entrance to the sanctuary, thus emphasizing the fact that they were entering the community. The symbols surrounding their baptisms dramatically emphasized that they were renouncing the powers of sin and death, pledging their loyalty to Christ, being washed and cleansed of sin, entering into the dying and rising of Christ, receiving a new identity, and entering into a new community of faith. All this was seen to be the gracious work of God, to which those who had received baptism would respond each day for the rest of their lives. Learning to live the Christian life was thus the responsibility both of the adults and of the children to whom baptism was given.

Immediately following baptism the new Christians were led to the center of the church, where each was anointed with oil (called chrism)[1] and received the laying on of hands. This service of anointing with oil included prayers that the Holy Spirit would "confirm" what the church had just done in baptism by living within the believer and empowering him or her to be a faithful Christian. Hence, anointing with oil was associated with the confirmation of the Holy Spirit and thus was always seen in relation to baptism.

Though baptism could be conferred only once, anointing with oil could be repeated again and again. Each time it brought believers in touch with the grace given in their baptisms and reminded them of the promises made. As such it was a renewal of baptism which the church encouraged its members to receive on many occasions: as preparation to receive the Lord's Supper, especially on the evening of great feasts such as Easter and Christmas; as a form of pastoral care for those who were troubled; and, above all, as part of the church's ministry to the sick and the dying.

After receiving baptism and confirmation the Christians, including infants, were welcomed to the Lord's Supper, the final sign that they had been fully received as members into the community.

In the Western church this unity of the three rites was broken by historical accidents. In the Roman or Latin church, only bishops were permitted to perform the anointing with oil. In the East, all three rites could be performed by priests. With the fall of Rome and the disintegration of the Western part of the empire, it became impossible for bishops to be present for all baptismal celebrations. Indeed, it was not uncommon to have years separating the event of baptism from the visit of the bishop. A very different pattern therefore developed, in which baptism was administered to infants, first communion to children, and confirmation when the child was recognized as having come of age. It is in large measure the loss of the unity of the relations of these three events which lies at the root of much of our confusion, since each came to exist in isolation and with theological explanations that only further obscured the simplicity and power of the sacraments themselves. Seen against this background, confirmation understandably now appears, in many of our churches, to be a rite in search of a theology. And the principal cause of this recent problem is that children are now being admitted to the Lord's Supper earlier than before, when confirmation could still be seen as itself the final preparation for being received at the Table.

Among many American Protestant churches engaged in the study and writing of new liturgical materials, there is a marked tendency to bring these three rites into relations that more closely parallel ancient practice. This is not simply a preference for that which is old, but rather the rediscovery of our common heritage in which ancient practice reveals the meanings of the rites themselves.

The new baptismal rite in this resource also moves in this direction, by reestablishing the relations between baptism and confirmation. It also encourages the church to bring baptized children to the Lord's Table as early as possible. The new rite not only contains the laying on of hands but also provides the option of anointing with oil, as the visible action signifying the sealing with the Holy Spirit of one who belongs to Christ. Indeed, the title *Christ* literally means "the anointed one." In time this may reopen the rich possibility for anointing the sick and dying and thus reestablishing lost connections to the continuing meaning of baptism in the Christian life. This of course will require careful interpretation. But it occurs when our church is already discovering its own need for a more compelling theology and practice of the sacraments.

Baptism and Personal Faith

In the pluralism and cross-fertilization of America's Protestant churches, many people have found themselves confronted with the long-standing conflict between Reformed Christians, on the one hand, and Anabaptists, on the other. Generally speaking, Christians of the Anabaptist tradition believe that scripture teaches that repentance must precede baptism and that baptism may be offered only to those who can profess personal faith. This of course presupposes cognition and awareness, which Anabaptists insist are essential prerequisites for baptism. Such a position clearly rules out any possibility of the baptism of infants.

The Reformed understanding of baptism has emphasized God's initiative. It is God who acts graciously in and through baptism, and it is we who respond and continue to do so for the rest of our lives. Since the days of John Calvin, this tradition has also viewed infants and children of believers as heirs to the covenant of grace. An infant or adult is baptized not only into the fellowship of a local congregation but also into the church universal. The Anabaptist insistence upon "understanding baptism" before receiving it poses enormous problems of establishing standards or criteria for what constitutes adequate knowledge, belief, or commitment. Would such criteria, for example, make it impossible for some mentally handicapped people to receive baptism? On what basis could general agreement about such issues be reached? In the Anabaptist tradition an emphasis is made upon the human response in baptism, while the Reformed tradition insists on God's sovereignty and gracious invitation to the unworthy and unqualified to receive the gift of the kingdom.

In addition, the baptism of some Anabaptist groups is viewed as an ordinance through which Christians enter into fellowship with a local congregation. Baptism is thus repeatable; indeed, it may be repeated each time a person seeks to become a member of a new congregation. In this understanding the church exists only as local congregations, each autonomous and complete in itself.

Such conflicts cannot be fully elaborated or resolved in this brief discussion. But this much can be said: For the Reformed tradition, whether we are five or fifty, we are all infants in the faith when we are baptized, and it is into the one holy catholic church that we enter by baptism.

Today we live in a secular society in which Christianity is waning in influence and adherents. Those "outside" the church cannot always identify characteristics of Christian living among the baptized that distinguish the baptized from the nonbaptized. It is entirely possible that the crisis of the church is really not qualitatively different from the baptismal crisis. The crisis of faith in which belief seems impossible, untenable, or irrelevant may be due in part to the fact that the baptismal realities of belonging to God, being transformed, dying, rising, being joined inextricably to a body of people whose lives are significantly different are sadly "invisible realities." Yet they are the ones which baptism and confirmation proclaim and of which they are themselves signs. The first step in addressing that crisis is to begin at the beginning, with a rite whose words and actions correspond more accurately and powerfully with the realities they describe. This is precisely what has been attempted in this new order for baptism.

AN ORDER FOR HOLY BAPTISM

BASIC STRUCTURE OF
AN ORDER FOR HOLY BAPTISM

PRESENTATION

Persons to be baptized are brought to the font and presented for baptism. The meaning of baptism is declared in the words of scripture. Older children, youth, and adults express their desire to be baptized. Parents promise to fulfill the responsibilities for Christian nurture. Sponsors promise to support those being baptized in their growth in the faith.

RENUNCIATION AND AFFIRMATION

Those coming to be baptized, parents, and sponsors make vows, renouncing the ways of evil and affirming the way of Christ. The congregation joins the candidates for baptism (or their parents) and the sponsors in affirming the faith of the church in the words of the Apostles' Creed.

THANKSGIVING OVER THE WATER

God's saving acts are remembered with thanksgiving and the Holy Spirit is invoked, that those who are baptized may have their sins washed away, be reborn to new life, be buried and resurrected with Christ, and be incorporated into the body of Christ.

THE ACT OF BAPTIZING

In the name of the triune God, the minister pours or sprinkles water visibly and generously on the head of each candidate or immerses each candidate in water.

THE BLESSING (AND ANOINTING)

As a sign of the gift of the Holy Spirit in baptism, the minister lays hands upon the head of the newly baptized (and may anoint with oil), praying for the gift of the Holy Spirit.

WELCOME

The congregation is reminded of its responsibility to love and nurture the new Christians and to assist them to be faithful disciples. The congregation welcomes the newly baptized into the household of God, sharing signs of peace.

OUTLINE OF THE SERVICE FOR THE LORD'S DAY INCLUDING THE SACRAMENT OF HOLY BAPTISM

ASSEMBLE IN GOD'S NAME

Gathering of the People
Call to Worship
Hymn of Praise, Psalm, or Spiritual
Confession and Pardon
Act of Praise

PROCLAIM GOD'S WORD

Prayer for Illumination
First Lesson
Psalm
Second Lesson
Hymn, Spiritual, or Anthem
Gospel Lesson
Sermon
Hymn, Psalm, or Spiritual
Holy Baptism
  Presentation
  Renunciation and Affirmation (including the Apostles' Creed)
  Thanksgiving Over the Water
  The Act of Baptizing
  The Blessing (and Anointing)
  Welcome
The Peace (optional)
Psalm, Hymn, or Spiritual
Prayers of Intercession
Offering

GIVE THANKS TO GOD

— *Or* —

Preparation of the Table	
Great Prayer of Thanksgiving, concluding with the Lord's Prayer	Prayer of Thanksgiving, concluding with the Lord's Prayer
Breaking of the Bread	
Communion of the People	

GO IN GOD'S NAME

Hymn, Spiritual, or Psalm
Charge and Blessing
Going Forth

AN ORDER FOR HOLY BAPTISM

PRESENTATION

Ordinarily, baptism is celebrated as part of the worship of the congregation on the Lord's Day, following the reading and preaching of the Word. An appropriate hymn, psalm, spiritual, or other suitable music may be sung while the candidates, sponsors, and parents assemble for baptism. The MINISTER addresses the baptismal group and the congregation:

Hear the words of Jesus:

All authority in heaven and on earth
has been given to me.
Go therefore and make disciples of all nations,
baptizing them in the name of the Father
and of the Son
and of the Holy Spirit,
teaching them to observe all that I have commanded you;
and lo, I am with you always,
to the close of the age. *Matt. 28:18–20*

The MINISTER continues, using one or more of the following:

Hear also these words from Holy Scripture:

There is one body and one Spirit,
just as you were called to the one hope
that belongs to your call,
one Lord, one faith, one baptism,
one God and Father of us all,
who is above all, and through all, and in all. *Eph. 4:4–6*

For as many of you as were baptized into Christ
have put on Christ.
There is neither Jew nor Greek,
there is neither slave nor free,
there is neither male nor female;
for you are all one in Christ Jesus. *Gal. 3:27–28*

You are a chosen race, a royal priesthood,
a holy nation, God's own people,
that you may declare the wonderful deeds of God,
who called you out of darkness
into God's marvelous light. *1 Peter 2:9*

Do you not know
that all of us who have been baptized into Christ Jesus
were baptized into his death?
We were buried therefore with him by baptism into death,
so that as Christ was raised from the dead
by the glory of the Father,
we too might walk in newness of life. *Rom. 6:3–4*

The promise is to you and to your children
and to all that are far off,
every one whom the Lord our God calls. *Acts 2:39*

The MINISTER continues:

Obeying the word of our Lord Jesus,
and confident of his promises,
we baptize those whom he has called.

In baptism God claims us,
and puts a sign on us to show that we belong to God.
God frees us from sin and death,
uniting us with Jesus Christ in his death and resurrection.
By water and the Holy Spirit,
we are made members of the church, the body of Christ,
and joined to Christ's ministry of love, peace, and justice.
Let us remember and rejoice in our own baptism,
as we celebrate this sacrament.

An ELDER presents each candidate for baptism:

On behalf of the session,
I present _____ to receive the sacrament of baptism.

ADULTS AND OLDER CHILDREN

The MINISTER addresses those candidates who are making their own profession of faith:

Do you desire to be baptized?

I do.

INFANTS AND YOUNGER CHILDREN

The MINISTER addresses the parent(s) of infants and younger children:

Do you desire that _____ be baptized?

I do.

Relying on God's grace,
do you promise to live the Christian faith
and to teach that faith to your child?

I do.

SPONSORS

The MINISTER addresses the sponsors, if any are present:

Do you promise, through prayer and example,
to support and encourage _____
to be a faithful Christian?

I do.

RENUNCIATION AND AFFIRMATION

The MINISTER asks the following questions of the candidates making a confession of faith, the parents, and the sponsors:

Through baptism we enter the covenant God has established.
Within that covenant we are given new life
and are guarded from evil,
nurtured by the love of God and God's people.
On our part, we are to turn from evil
and turn to Jesus Christ.

I ask you, therefore,
to reject sin,
to profess your faith in Christ Jesus,
and to confess the faith of the church,
the faith in which we baptize.

Do you renounce evil,
and its power in the world,
which defies God's righteousness and love?

I renounce them.

Do you renounce the ways of sin
that separate you from the love of God?

I renounce them.

Do you turn to Jesus Christ
and accept him as your Lord and Savior?

I do.

Do you intend to be Christ's faithful disciple,
obeying his word, and showing his love,
to your life's end?

I do.

With the whole church,
let us confess our faith.

> *The CONGREGATION stands and remains standing throughout the
> rest of the rite. The CONGREGATION, the CANDIDATES (or their
> PARENTS), and SPONSORS join in affirming the faith in the words
> of the Apostles' Creed. The questions may be deleted when pastoral
> considerations make it necessary.*

Do you believe in God the Father?

**I believe in God, the Father almighty,
creator of heaven and earth.**

Do you believe in Jesus Christ, the Son of God?

I believe in Jesus Christ, his only Son, our Lord.
He was conceived by the power of the Holy Spirit
and born of the Virgin Mary.
He suffered under Pontius Pilate,
was crucified, died, and was buried.
He descended to the dead.
On the third day he rose again.
He ascended into heaven,
and is seated at the right hand of the Father.
He will come again to judge the living and the dead.

Do you believe in God the Holy Spirit?

I believe in the Holy Spirit,
the holy catholic church,
the communion of saints,
the forgiveness of sins,
the resurrection of the body,
and the life everlasting. Amen.

Water is poured into the font at this time.

Thanksgiving Over the Water

The MINISTER says:

The Lord be with you.

And also with you.

Let us give thanks to the Lord our God.

It is right to give our thanks and praise.

We give you thanks,
O holy and gracious God,
for in the beginning your Spirit moved over the water,
and you created all that is, seen and unseen.
By the gift of water you sustain all life.

In the time of Noah,
you destroyed evil in the water of the flood;
and by your saving ark, you gave a new beginning.
You led Israel through the sea,
out of slavery into the freedom of the promised land.

In the water of Jordan
our Lord was baptized by John
and anointed by your Spirit.
By the baptism of his death and resurrection,
Christ set us free from sin and death
and opened the way to eternal life.

We thank you, O God, for the gift of baptism.
In this water we are buried with Christ in his death.
From this water we are raised to share in his resurrection,
reborn by the power of the Holy Spirit.

The MINISTER may touch the water.

By the power of your Spirit, bless this water,
that it may be a fountain of deliverance and rebirth.
Wash away the sins of *all* who *are* cleansed by it.
Raise *them* to new life,
and graft *them* to the body of Christ.
Pour out your Holy Spirit upon *them*,
that *they* may have power to do your will,
and continue forever in the risen life of Christ,
to whom, with the Father and the Holy Spirit,
be all glory and honor,
now and forever.

Amen.

THE ACT OF BAPTIZING

The congregation remains standing for the act of baptizing.

Calling each candidate by his or her Christian (given) name or names, the MINISTER pours or sprinkles water visibly and generously on the candidate's head, or immerses the candidate, while saying:

_____, I baptize you
in the name of the Father,
and of the Son,
and of the Holy Spirit.

Amen.

THE BLESSING (AND ANOINTING)

The MINISTER lays hands on the head of the person baptized while saying:

O Lord, uphold _____ by your Holy Spirit.
Give *(him, her)* the spirit of wisdom and understanding,
the spirit of counsel and might,
the spirit of knowledge and the fear of the Lord,
the spirit of joy in your presence,
both now and forever.

Amen.

As the MINISTER says these words, the sign of the cross may be marked on the forehead of the person baptized, using oil prepared for this purpose:

_____, child of the covenant,
you have been sealed by the Holy Spirit in baptism,
and marked as Christ's own forever.

Amen.

WELCOME

A REPRESENTATIVE OF THE SESSION, or the MINISTER,
addresses the congregation in these or similar words:

_____, _____ *are* now received into the holy catholic church.
Through baptism God has made *them members* of the
household of God,
to share with us in the priesthood of Christ.
I charge you, the people of this congregation,
to nurture and to love *them,*
and to assist *them* to be faithful *disciples.*

The CONGREGATION responds:

With joy and thanksgiving,
we welcome you into Christ's church;
for we are all one in Christ.
We promise to love, encourage, and support you,
to share the good news of the gospel with you,
and to help you know and follow Christ.

The peace of God be with you.

And also with you.

The CONGREGATION may exchange signs of God's peace, greeting
those who have been baptized.

An appropriate psalm, hymn, or spiritual may be sung as all return
to their places.

The service continues with the Prayers of Intercession, which will
include petitions for the newly baptized and for those who will nurture
them (pp. 42–43).

When the Lord's Supper is celebrated, it is appropriate for the newly
baptized to receive communion first.

ALTERNATE LITURGICAL TEXTS

This section provides liturgical texts that may be substituted for portions of the baptismal rite.

RENUNCIATION AND AFFIRMATION

A.

The following question may replace the first two questions in the section "Renunciation and Affirmation" (p. 28), with no change to the rest of that section of the rite.

Do you renounce sin and the power of evil
in your life and in the world?

I do.

B.

One of the following may be added after any statement of renunciation in order to contemporize the candidate's understanding of evil as any destructive force, such as racism, sexism, greed, or economic exploitation (see p. 52).

Do you renounce any thought or behavior that does not bear witness to the wholeness of the body of Christ?

I do.

Or

Do you renounce any thought, word, or deed that would prevent you from exemplifying true Christian discipleship?

I do.

C.

The following question may replace the four questions that precede the Apostles' Creed in the section "Renunciation and Affirmation" (p. 28). This question is based upon the exhortations in the baptismal rite of John Calvin.[2] Renunciation and affirmation are combined in one question.

Do you renounce your own sinful desires,
and pledge to devote yourself to glorify the name of God
and to love your neighbor?

I do.

D.

The following question may replace the third and fourth questions in the section "Renunciation and Affirmation" (p. 28).

Who is your Lord and Savior?

Jesus Christ is my Lord and Savior.

Will you be Christ's faithful disciple,
obeying his word and showing his love?

I will, through God's grace.

THANKSGIVING OVER THE WATER

A.

While this prayer may be used in any baptism, it is particularly appropriate for use in the Easter vigil and other festival occasions. The prayer includes congregational responses, which may be sung or said. If the responses are impractical, they may be omitted.

The Lord be with you.

And also with you.

Let us give thanks to the Lord our God.

It is right to give our thanks and praise.

O holy, almighty, and most gracious God,
you reign over all creation.
In you alone we find life.
By your power we are upheld.

Your mercy and love endure forever.

We give you thanks,
for in the beginning,
your Spirit swept across the watery chaos,
and order and life were called forth.
By the gift of water,
you nourish and sustain all living things.

Your mercy and love endure forever.

In the water of the flood, you destroyed evil,
but gave righteousness a new beginning,
by saving Noah and his family, who found favor in your sight.

Your mercy and love endure forever.

By the pillar of cloud and fire,
you led Israel through the water of the sea,
out of slavery into freedom.
Across the water of Jordan,
you brought your chosen ones into the land of your promise.

Your mercy and love endure forever.

In the water of the Jordan,
Jesus was baptized by John
and anointed with the Spirit.
By the baptism of his death,
he set us free from bondage to sin and death.
By his resurrection,
he opened the way to eternal life.

Your mercy and love endure forever.

We praise you, O God,
for the countless ways you have revealed yourself in ages past
and for the signs of your grace you have given us.

Your mercy and love endure forever.

And now, at this new beginning,
we thank you for the gift of baptism.
In this water we are buried with Christ in his death;
from this water we are raised to share in his resurrection;
through this water we are reborn by the power of the Holy Spirit.

Your mercy and love endure forever.

   The MINISTER may touch the water.

By the power of your Spirit, bless this water,
that it may be a fountain of deliverance and rebirth.
Wash away the sins of *all* who *are* cleansed by it.
Raise *them* to new life
and graft *them* to the body of Christ.
Pour out your Holy Spirit upon *them*,
that *they* may have power to do your will,
and continue forever in the risen life of Christ,
to whom, with the Father and the Holy Spirit,
be all glory and honor,
now and forever.

Amen.

B.

If desired, the dialogue that begins the other thanksgivings over the water may be added to the following prayer:

Eternal and gracious God, we give you thanks.
Through the water of the sea,
you led your people Israel out of slavery
into the freedom of the land of your promise.
In the water of the Jordan,
your Son was baptized
and anointed by the Holy Spirit.
Through the baptism of Jesus' death and resurrection,
you set us free from the bondage of sin and death
and give us cleansing and rebirth.

We praise you, almighty God,
for new beginnings in this water of baptism.

The MINISTER may touch the water.

By the power of your Holy Spirit, bless this water.
Grant that *those* who *are* washed in this water
may be cleansed of sin and born anew.
Bind *them* to the household of faith
and guard *them* from all evil.
Pour out your Spirit upon *them,*
that *they* may be strengthened to serve you with joy,
until that day when you make all things new.
To you, Father, Son, and Holy Spirit, one God,
be all praise, honor, and glory,
now and forever.

Amen.

THE ACT OF BAPTIZING

Two alternatives to the traditional Western formula (p. 31) are provided. Each, like the Western wording, includes the necessary phrase "in the name of the Father, and of the Son, and of the Holy Spirit," but varies in other aspects.

Alternate A is based upon the Western formula but adds "child of the covenant." It was included in "The Directory for the Worship and Work of the Church" of the former Presbyterian Church in the United States.

Alternate B is the formula used in the Eastern tradition.

A.
_____, child of the covenant,
I baptize you
in the name of the Father,
and of the Son,
and of the Holy Spirit.

Amen.

B.
_____ is baptized
in the name of the Father,
and of the Son,
and of the Holy Spirit.

Amen.

38   *Alternate Liturgical Texts*

The Blessing (and Anointing)

The MINISTER lays hands on the head of the person baptized while saying:

Defend, O Lord, your servant _____
with your heavenly grace,
that *(he, she)* may continue yours forever,
and daily increase in your Holy Spirit more and more,
until *(he, she)* comes to your everlasting kingdom.

Amen.

As the MINISTER says these words, the sign of the cross may be marked on the forehead of the person baptized, using oil prepared for this purpose.

_____, child of God,
you have been sealed by the Holy Spirit in baptism,
and grafted into Christ forever.

Amen.

LITURGICAL TEXTS FOR A SERVICE IN WHICH A BAPTISM IS CELEBRATED

Baptism is particularly appropriate in the Easter vigil, the Sundays of Easter, Pentecost Sunday, All Saints' Day, and the Baptism of the Lord (the first Sunday after Epiphany). Liturgical texts for these times focus upon those biblical events which are the basis of baptism. Consequently, no other liturgical texts that relate to baptism are needed. When baptism is celebrated at other times, liturgical texts that relate to baptism may be desired. The Service for the Lord's Day (Supplemental Liturgical Resource 1) contains many texts that are appropriate for the celebration of baptism. Other appropriate texts are included here.

SENTENCES FROM SCRIPTURE FOR THE CALL TO WORSHIP

Verses of scripture that are options in the beginning of the baptismal rite (pp. 25–26), and that will not be used in the baptism, may be used as a call to worship. Other appropriate scripture texts are as follows:

1.

Ask, and you will receive;
seek, and you will find;
knock, and the door will be opened to you.   *Matt. 7:7; Luke 11:9*

2.

For just as the body is one
and has many members,
and all the members of the body, though many,
are one body,
so it is with Christ.

For by one Spirit
we were all baptized into one body—
Jews or Greeks, slaves or free—
and all were made to drink of one Spirit.

Now you are the body of Christ
and individually members of it.   *1 Cor. 12:12–13, 27*

3.
Jesus said:
Unless we are born anew,
we cannot see the kingdom of God.
Unless we are born of water and the Spirit,
we cannot enter the kingdom of God. *John 3:3, 5*

4.
Jesus said:
I am the light of the world;
those who follow me will not walk in darkness,
but will have the light of life. *John 8:12*

5.
Jesus said:
I am the way, and the truth, and the life;
no one comes to the Father, but by me. *John 14:6*

6.
In baptism we were buried with Christ.
In baptism also we were raised to life with him
through faith in the power of God
who raised him from the dead. *Col. 2:12*

If then you have been raised with Christ,
seek the things that are above,
where Christ is, seated at the right hand of God. *Col. 3:1*

7.
See what love God has given us,
that we should be called children of God;
and so we are. *1 John 3:1*

DECLARATION OF PARDON

Once you were no people
but now you are God's people;
once you had not received mercy
but now you have received mercy. *1 Peter 2:10*

In Christ you are forgiven.

Glory to God. Amen.

Blessed be God for ever and ever.
By God's great mercy
we have been born anew to a living hope
through the resurrection of Jesus Christ from the dead,
and to an inheritance
which nothing can destroy or spoil or wither.
It is kept for us in heaven,
and will be revealed at the end of time.
We rejoice with a joy too great for words.   *1 Peter 1:3–5*

PRAYERS OF INTERCESSION

FOR THE NEWLY BAPTIZED AND NEW MEMBERS

Merciful God, you call us by name
and promise to each of us your constant love.
Watch over your *servants* _____, _____.
Deepen *their* understanding of the gospel,
strengthen *their* commitment to follow the way of Christ,
and keep *them* in the faith and communion of your church.
Increase *their* compassion for others,
send *them* into the world in witness to your love,
and bring *them* to the fullness of your peace and glory,
through Jesus Christ our Lord.

Amen.

FOR PARENTS WHOSE CHILDREN HAVE JUST BEEN BAPTIZED

Gracious God, giver of all life,
We pray for *parents* _____, _____.
Give *them* wisdom and patience
to guide *their children* in the way of Jesus Christ
and the faith of the church.
Let your peace and joy dwell in *their* home,
that *their* family life may be instructed by faith,
sustained by prayer, and governed by love.
Strengthen *them* in *their* own baptism,

that *they* may rejoice as *children* of God,
and serve you faithfully,
in the name of Jesus Christ.

Amen.

FOR NEWLY BAPTIZED INFANTS AND CHILDREN

Ever-living God,
in your mercy you promised to be not only our God
but also the God of our children.
We thank you for receiving _____, _____ by baptism.
Keep *them* always in your love.
Guide *them* as *they grow* in faith.
Protect *them* in all the dangers and temptations of life.
Bring *them* to confess Jesus Christ as *their* Lord and Savior
and be his faithful *disciples* to *their* life's end,
in the name of Jesus Christ.

Amen.

FOR FAMILIES

Loving God,
you nurture and guide us like a father and mother.
We pray for the families of this congregation,
and for all Christian families everywhere.
Give them strength to honor you in their homes,
and to love and serve each other.
Help all who have been baptized in your name
to live in peace and unity,
as sisters and brothers in the household of faith,
and to serve others in the name of Jesus Christ.

Amen.

CHARGE

You are a chosen race, a royal priesthood,
a holy nation, God's own people,
that you may declare the wonderful deeds of God,
who called you out of darkness
into God's marvelous light.   *1 Peter 2:9*

MUSIC FOR BAPTISM

The following music is appropriate for baptism:

HYMNS

	Hymnbook	Worshipbook
Blessed Jesus, We Are Here		310
Come Down, O Love Divine		334
O God, This Child from You Did Come		501
Descend, O Spirit, Purging Flame		353
Father, We Thank You that You Planted		366
Jesus, Friend, So Kind and Gentle	451	
Lord Jesus Christ, Our Lord Most Dear	452	461
Pardoned Through Redeeming Grace		550

OCTAVOS

	Author	Publisher
You Have Put on Christ	Howard Hughes	G.I.A.
Little Children, Welcome	Hal Hopson	Agape

PSALMS

Of the resources listed, GG is *The Gelineau Gradual* (G-2124, G.I.A. Publications, 7404 South Mason Avenue, Chicago, IL 60638) and GP is *Gradual Psalms* (Church Hymnal Corp., 800 Second Avenue, New York, NY 10017).

Psalm 8

O Lord, Our Lord, in All the Earth (metrical)	*Hymnbook* 95; *Worshipbook* 515
When I See the Heavens (Gelineau)	GG p. 141
Gregorian psalm tone	GP (Thursday Easter Week)

Psalm 23

The Lord's My Shepherd (metrical)	*Hymnbook* 104 (2nd tune)
The Lord's My Shepherd (Gelineau)	GG p. 136
Gregorian psalm tone	GP (Year A, Proper 23)

Psalm 29

God the Omnipotent! (metrical-free paraphrase)	*Hymnbook* 487
O Give the Lord, You Sons of God (Gelineau)	GG p. 20
Gregorian psalm tone	GP (Year A, Proper 14)

Psalm 32

How Blest Is He Whose Trespass
(metrical)   *Hymnbook* 281
Happy the Man Whose Offence Is
Forgiven (Gelineau)   GG p. 86
Gregorian psalm tone   GP (Year B, Epiphany 7)

Psalm 42

As Pants the Hart for Cooling Streams
(metrical)   *Hymnbook* 322
My Soul Is Thirsting for God (Gelineau)   GG p. 44
Gregorian psalm tone   GP (Easter vigil,
                                        Years A, B, C)

Psalm 43:3–4

Gregorian psalm tone   GP (Maundy Thursday,
                                        Years A, B, C)

Psalm 51:1–17

God, Be Merciful to Me (metrical)   *Hymnbook* 282
Have Mercy on Me, God   GG, p. 34
Gregorian psalm tone   GP (Year B, 5 Lent)

Psalm 63:2–8

O Lord, My God, Most Earnestly   *Hymnbook* 327
                                    Worshipbook 514
O God, You Are My God (Gelineau)   GG, p. 132
Gregorian psalm tone   GP (Year B, Epiphany 2)

Psalm 103

Bless, O My Soul! The Living God
(metrical)   *Hymnbook* 8
My Soul, Give Thanks to the Lord
(Gelineau)   GG, p. 77
Gregorian psalm tone   GP (Year C, 3 Lent)

Psalm 116

What Shall I Render to the Lord
(metrical)   *Hymnbook* 32
I Trusted, Even When I Said (Gelineau)   GG, p. 25
Gregorian psalm tone   GP (Year B, 3 Easter)

HYMNS FROM ASIAN-AMERICAN TRADITIONS

These hymns are taken from *Hymns from the Four Winds (Supplemental Worship Resources 13;*United Methodist Church, Abingdon Press, 1983).

Chinese

Every Day, Every Hour	109
Gentle Jesus, Meek and Mild	97
Jesus Loved Each Little Child	98

Japanese

A Grain of Wheat	107
Climb On, Climb On, Young Friend	107

Philippine

Dear Lord, Lead Me Day by Day	96

(East) Indian

O Praise the Lord (Trinitarian)	15

Korean

Drawing Near and List'ning	62
Living with the Lord	77

Songs of Baptism from the Afro-American Tradition

Of the resources listed, SZ is *Songs of Zion (Supplemental Worship Resources 12;* Abingdon Press, 1981) and YL is *Yes, Lord* (Church of God in Christ Hymnal; Benson Company, Memphis, TN 38126 or Nashville, TN 37228).

Cert'nly Lord (Have You Been Baptized? and/or Certainly, Lord)	SZ 161 *or* Carl Fisher CM 6641, Hall Johnson arrangement *or* Kjos ED5458, Lena McLin arrangement
Honor, Honor (King Jesus lit the candle by the waterside to see the little children when they're truly baptized, Honor, Honor, unto the dying Lamb . . . Oh, run along children, "Be baptized, mighty pretty meeting by the waterside . . ."	Carl Fisher CM21826 (SATB), Hall Johnson arrangement (check catalogs for others)
Pray On! (In the river of Jordan John baptized)	John W. Work, *American Negro Songs and Spirituals,* p. 81
Take Me to the Water (to be baptized)	YL 349
Wade in the Water	SZ 129
'Jus Come from the Fountain	YL 365
Live a-Humble	SZ 108 *or* Schumann S-1020, Jester Hairston arrangement
Lord, I Want to Be a Christian	*Hymnbook* 317

COMMENTARY ON
AN ORDER FOR HOLY BAPTISM

The commentary that follows provides users of this resource with a rationale for the order set forth on pages 22–32 and offers suggestions for its use. Users of this baptismal rite are also directed to the "Proposed Chapter on Baptism for a New Directory for Worship," received for study by the 196th General Assembly (1984) of the Presbyterian Church (U.S.A.), and the commentary that accompanies it. The chapter (hereafter referred to as Proposed Chapter) and commentary will contribute to an understanding of the baptismal liturgy included in this resource.[3]

One Baptismal Rite

Only one order for baptism is provided. The precedent for this was established by *The Worshipbook* in its provision of only one baptismal rite to be used with persons of all ages. Baptism is the same sacrament whether the person being baptized is an infant, child, youth, or adult.

The Place and Time for Baptism

Although baptism is personal, it is also a communal sacrament, since baptism incorporates one into the community of faith. For this reason, baptism ordinarily is celebrated in the midst of the worshiping congregation.[4] The congregation should have an opportunity to be part of the celebration and welcome the new members of the body of Christ. It is because of this communal character that the Reformers opposed private baptism. Moreover, except for extraordinary circumstances, baptism takes place in the congregation where it is expected the person being baptized will be nurtured.

Early in the church's history, baptism usually occurred in the annual Easter vigil on the Saturday night before Easter Day, the culmination of a long period of preparation and teaching. As part of the Easter celebration, baptism was clearly related to Christ's death and resurrection.[5]

While it is appropriate to celebrate baptism on any Lord's Day, other times in the liturgical year are especially significant times for baptism. The Easter vigil has already been mentioned. Other significant occasions include Baptism of the Lord (the first Sunday after Epiphany), the Sundays of Easter, Pentecost Sunday, and All Saints' Day. Celebrating baptism on these occasions proclaims that our life as Christians is rooted in the mighty acts of God in Jesus Christ.

The Place for Baptism in the Service

Baptism most appropriately follows the reading and preaching of the Word, for they provide the occasion for instructing in the meaning of baptism out of the mystery of God's Word. Furthermore, God's prior grace and continued faithfulness are emphasized, since presenting ourselves or our children for baptism is a response to God's grace made known in scripture and declared in preaching.

Presentation

The person to be baptized is presented by an elder. Regardless of the candidate's age or situation, each is presented. This act of presentation makes it clear that no one presumes to *come* to baptism but is presented by a representative of the community of faith.

The presentation begins with a gathering at the font. This may include a procession to the font during the singing of a psalm (Psalms 8, 23, 29, 32, 42:1–3 with 43:3–4, 51:1–17, 63:2–8, 103, and 116 are particularly appropriate when baptism is celebrated), hymn, or spiritual.[6] If space permits, the entire congregation may assemble about the font.

The minister, acting on behalf of the universal church, presides at the baptism. After the baptismal group has assembled, the minister reads verses from scripture that express the meaning of baptism. Some of the varied meanings are then summarized. Texts are provided in this resource.

Sponsors

The Proposed Chapter opens the way for including sponsors in the baptismal service when it states, "The session, in consultation with those desiring baptism for themselves or their child, may appoint additional sponsors charged on behalf of the congregation and of the church universal with particular responsibility for the Christian nurture of the baptized person."[7]

Sponsors are Christian persons who accept a particular responsibility for the spiritual nurture of those to be baptized. Their presence emphasizes that baptism is integral to the life of the Christian community and that the congregation has a serious obligation to nurture those it baptizes. There may be sponsors for adults as well as for young children. The Reformed tradition has always emphasized that the entire congregation serves as the sponsor for those baptized. The appointment of individuals as sponsors does not deemphasize the role of the session and congregation in nurturing the baptized but rather seeks to give it functional and personal expression.

Sponsors are appointed by the session, which needs to exercise care in their appointment. Sponsors need to be baptized, practicing Christians, preferably members of the congregation in which the baptized person will participate. Before sessional approval is given, persons should be instructed in and joyfully accept their responsibility. Moreover, the role of sponsors is more than participating in the baptism. Sponsors are to help nurture the new Christians as they are incorporated into the church. This responsibility continues throughout life.

The Name of the Candidate

The name of the candidate is announced by an elder as part of the presentation. The use of a person's name in baptism is its most important use in all of the Christian liturgy, for it marks adoption into the family of God. One's name is an extension of one's identity, a sign of one's uniqueness as a human being.

Accepting Responsibility for Baptism

Two questions are asked of the parent(s) presenting children for baptism. In these questions the church seeks to be assured that infants and children being baptized will be nurtured in the faith so that they may grow to spiritual maturity. Christian nurture takes place where the parent(s) care for the spiritual well-being of their children as carefully as they do their physical health.

Candidates old enough to make decisions are asked to express their desire for baptism. No one is coerced into being baptized.

The sponsors are also asked to commit themselves to the support of the newly baptized as they grow in faith.

The rite may be adapted to accommodate those who are old enough to profess faith appropriate to their age level (perhaps ages four to eleven) and who express a desire for baptism, but who are not yet old enough to assume all the responsibilities of church membership. Such an adaptation would include the questions directed to the parent(s) *and* those directed to the candidate.

Renunciation and Affirmation

The Christian life involves both a *turning from* sin and bondage to evil and a *turning to* Christ and the way of righteousness. It is to turn our backs on the kind of life that is destructive and to embrace the new life that is promised in the gospel. Both renunciation and affirmation are aspects of the Christian life, and therefore they are important aspects of the baptismal liturgy. Both are equally dependent upon God's grace active in our lives and in the community of faith.

In apostolic times, as evidenced in the Acts of the Apostles, candidates for baptism expressed their faith in Christ before the washing with water. From as early as the third century, the baptismal rite included a twofold profession of faith, in which the candidates, upon entering the water, were asked to "renounce Satan, and all his works" and to confess Christ.

In the ancient church this was expressed in a dramatic way. Immediately before baptism, candidates were asked to turn and, while facing west, to renounce evil. The west, as the place of the setting sun and gathering darkness, symbolized the abode of evil. The candidates then turned to the east and professed the Christian faith. The east, the place of the rising sun, was symbolic of Christ, the Light of the World. At that time church buildings were laid out so that the altar was in the east end of the worship space. Therefore, those early Christians literally turned their backs on the ways of Satan and his darkness as they faced the altar and affirmed the ways of Christ.

In keeping with the dual aspects of faith profession, the Proposed Chapter appropriately states that those desiring baptism shall, in professing their faith, "renounce evil and affirm their reliance on God's grace."[8]

Renunciation

Renunciation marks the ethical change that is implicit in the Christian life (e.g., Col. 3:8–10; 1 Peter 3:18–22). Turning from evil is part of one's faith commitment, because Christian discipleship is a way of life that contrasts with the ways of death, which prevail in the world.

The age in which we live is no exception to the need to renounce evil. Both in personal life and in the life of society, destructive forces are at work, forces such as greed, lust, selfishness, pride, materialism, militarism, racism, sexism, and economic exploitation.

The renunciation of evil in the baptismal liturgy reminds us that turning from sin is a critical aspect of discipleship and continues throughout the Christian's life. Since the baptismal liturgy marks the beginning of the Christian life and focuses upon the life Christians are to live, the renunciation is appropriate even in the baptism of infants.

Affirmation

In turning *from* evil, Christians turn *to* the way of the gospel. To profess faith is to affirm that as Christians we live out of a particular stance of faith. Personal faith is rooted in the faith of the church and is therefore expressed in baptism within the context of the faith of the church.

The oldest surviving baptismal liturgy, dating from around the year A.D. 200 (Hippolytus), describes the candidate standing in the water and affirming the faith by responding to three questions, each centering on a person of the Trinity. To each question the candidate responds, "I believe," and after each response is immersed in the water. The candidate's profession of faith was made in the context of articulation of the faith into which the new Christian was entering, and by which he or she would be refashioned.

This ancient pattern of baptismal vows is the basis for the Apostles' Creed. For many centuries the Apostles' Creed has been dominant in the baptismal rites of the West. As an ecumenical creed it summarizes the faith of the church, acknowledging that we are baptized into the one holy catholic church.

The Apostles' Creed is especially appropriate for use in baptism and is therefore recommended over other creedal statements. As an ecumenical creed it summarizes the faith of the whole church, linking the particular baptism with the believing community throughout history. Baptism is not an occasion for using a statement of faith that is sectarian or local in nature, for we are baptized into the universal faith. To show that personal faith is not separate from the church's faith, the entire congregation says the creed in the baptismal rite.

The interrogative form of the creed (pp. 28–29) is in keeping with the most ancient form of the Apostles' Creed noted above. Use of this particular form is therefore a desirable way to express the historic and universal faith of the church. It is now the form that is used in baptism in many branches of the church.

Thanksgiving Over the Water

Water is the primary and essential symbol in baptism. In early civilizations, water was regarded as one of the four basic elements in the universe, and it is still a powerful symbol for us today. Water is basic to life. Before each of us was born it protected us in our mother's womb. We cleanse our bodies with it. It brings cooling refreshment. It sustains life on our planet. Without water we will die. But by it we may die, for water also has power to kill. We can drown in it. Floods destroy life and property. This is why water speaks so forcefully in baptism when used in abundance.

The power of the symbolism of water is particularly dramatic where there is a baptismal pool or font which is kept full of flowing water. Throughout history the place of baptism has been regarded as a *bath* by which we are cleansed of sin, a *womb* from which we are reborn, a *tomb* in which we are buried with Christ and from which we are raised with him. This is more readily apparent when the baptismal space is ample and the baptismal font or pool is in a prominent location.

In early history when baptisms were by immersion, no particular care was needed to emphasize the power and centrality of water in baptism. But in our day fonts have become so small they are no longer able to hold enough water to symbolize its meaning and power.[9]

In cases where the font must be filled before the baptism, the centrality of the water is heightened if the font is filled as a part of the baptismal service. Water may be poured into the font from a ewer, or large pitcher, held high enough above the font so that the falling water may be seen by all, and the sounds of its splashing may be heard. An appropriate time for this action to take place is immediately before the thanksgiving over the water.

Prayer Over the Water
The Proposed Chapter states, "The minister of Word and Sacrament shall offer a baptismal prayer. This prayer shall express thanksgiving for God's covenant faithfulness and shall give praise for God's

reconciling acts. The prayer shall ask that the Holy Spirit attend and empower the rite, make the water a water of redemption and rebirth, and equip the church for faithfulness."[10]

In this prayer, so central to the act of baptism, God's saving acts are recalled with thanksgiving and the Holy Spirit is invoked, to the end that those who are baptized may have their sins washed away, be reborn to new life, be buried and resurrected with Christ, and be incorporated into the body of Christ.

This prayer is parallel to the great prayer of thanksgiving of the Lord's Supper. It is just as essential to baptism as its counterpart is to the Eucharist. The people stand for this act of praise and proclamation just as they do for the eucharistic thanksgiving.

Examples of this prayer, both ancient and modern, include rich biblical images of baptism and have a consistent form. Images incorporated are the waters of creation, the flood, the exodus, and the baptism of Jesus. The Spirit is then invoked, that those who are baptized may receive the new life promised in the gospel. "The prayer roots our story in the story of God's dealings with humanity and points us forward in hope to the new creation. Just as 'the Spirit of God moved upon the face of the waters' (Gen. 1:2) of creation's beginning, bringing order out of chaos, in the waters of Baptism the Spirit of God is recreating all things new."[11]

Touching the water is a gesture that is as natural here as it is for the minister to pick up the bread and the chalice when repeating the words of institution in the Lord's Supper. This action emphasizes the physical element of the sacrament and adds drama to the action.

The Act of Baptizing

The washing with water in the name of the triune God is at the heart of the sacrament, both theologically and dramatically. The Proposed Chapter states, "Water shall be applied to the person by pouring, sprinkling, or immersion. By whatever mode, the water should be applied visibly and generously."[12]

In the early centuries, baptism was usually by immersion. However, this need not have meant full submersion in the water. Early Christian mosaics portray persons kneeling or standing in the baptismal pool with water being poured over them. Whatever the practice, baptism connoted going down into the water and coming up out of the water. In later centuries, when the baptism of adults was rare, fonts were still large enough to immerse infants. Eastern Orthodox churches continue to immerse infants to the present day. For a variety of reasons, this practice did not continue in most of the Western churches.

While the quantity of water applied in baptism does not affect the validity of the sacrament, it does enhance the ability of the sacrament to express that of which it is a sign. God speaks to us not only through our minds but through our bodies and senses as well. The water of baptism can speak with great power in ways that words alone cannot. More is needed than a few drops of water to express the power of water in baptism. Whatever the mode, "let enough water be used so that the one being baptized gets wet, and all who are gathered can see the water and hear it splash. It will speak of washing, death, the giving and sustaining of life, refreshment, creation. We lose that impact when minimalism shapes liturgy."[13] It is crucial to the integrity of baptism that water once again be used "visibly and generously."

Three modes of baptism are suggested. Each mode has roots in scripture and has found a place in baptismal tradition. Each has been strongly defended.[14]

In recent years, however, there is an increased desire to restore the centrality of water in our baptismal rites. Immersion clearly does that. When immersion is not used, the preferable mode is to pour water over the head of the person being baptized. As in ancient practice, water may be poured over the head three times as the triune name of God is spoken.

In the Name of the Triune God

Christian baptism is "in the name of the Father and of the Son and of the Holy Spirit," in fulfillment of the command of the risen Christ (Matt. 28:19). Grounded in scripture, this formula has been used throughout Christian history in the initiation of Christians into the community of faith. All branches of the church regard this formula and the use of water as the essentials of a valid baptism. These words thereby mark "the one baptism" that unites all Christians in the one holy catholic and apostolic church. No other words can link us with this heritage or maintain our unity with the rest of the church. Today, many in the church have raised serious questions about the trinitarian formula with respect to its gender-specific character and its roots in ancient theological controversies and language. Although the church continues to struggle with this issue, the trinitarian formula remains essential to Christian baptism.[15]

Both the Proposed Chapter and the liturgy in this resource state that the *given* name is to be used in baptism. Traditionally, the surname, or family name, is not used. In the West it was long regarded that a person's name was officially bestowed at baptism, hence the common reference to one's "baptismal name" or "Christian name." Certainly baptism is more than bestowing a name, but there is significance in using the name given the person, without the family name. In baptism we are reborn into a new family, baptized into the surname of the triune God. Beginning with baptism we bear that surname. Baptized, we are sisters and brothers together in a family that transcends the family of our physical birth. This understanding is implicit when in baptism, as at other times in the church's liturgy, only the given name is used.

The Blessing (and Anointing)

The Proposed Chapter and the baptism service in this resource open up other ceremonial possibilities than those customarily included in Reformed baptism.[16] There is theological significance in the enrichment of the baptismal rite with certain ancient actions. The most significant possibilities occur immediately after the washing with water.

Laying On of Hands

The Proposed Chapter suggests the possible addition of the laying on of hands and a prayer for the gift of the Spirit. In the rite, such a prayer is preceded with a rubric that says that "the MINISTER lays hands on the head of the person baptized while saying" the prayer.

The laying on of hands appears many times in the Bible as a solemn act of blessing. In the Acts of the Apostles it is associated with baptism. As the baptismal liturgy developed in Christian history, the laying on of hands came to be related to the gifts of the Holy Spirit.

Anointing

By at least the third century, anointing with chrism[17] accompanied the laying on of hands in the baptismal liturgy. In the West, the laying on of hands and anointing with chrism were separated from baptism and became the rite of confirmation.[18] In the East, this division never occurred. Some contemporary baptismal rites evidence a movement to restore the laying on of hands and anointing with chrism to the baptismal rite. In these rites, the gift of the Holy Spirit in baptism is once more signified by these ancient signs. While baptism with water needs nothing to complete it, the laying on of hands and anointing help to convey the richness and abundance of the Holy Spirit and to demonstrate that Christian baptism is a baptism with water *and* the Holy Spirit. The early church developed this ritual based upon the baptism of Jesus, on whom the Holy Spirit descended as he emerged from the waters of the Jordan.

Anointing with chrism has a very ancient origin and was assimilated by the early Christians from Old Testament times. In ancient Israel it was associated with the anointing of kings and priests. So also, as God's baptized and Spirit-filled people, we share in the priesthood and rule of Christ, the Anointed One (Rev. 1:6; 5:10; 1 Peter 2:5, 9). "The anointing with chrism is a literalizing of New Testament imagery (1 John 2:20; 2 Cor. 1:21, 22; Eph. 1:13, 14; see also 1 Peter 2:9 and John 3:3–6) and is a sign of the meaning of the name 'Christian' (both *Christian* and *chrism*, as their similarity in sound implies, derive from the same Greek root, translated Christ meaning 'the anointed one'). The anointing of new Christians emphasizes their union with Jesus the Christ and their claim to the name 'Christian.' . . . The act of anointing is therefore particularly illustrative of one's 'taking the name of Christ' in Baptism."[19]

If candidates are to be anointed with oil, the procedure is for the minister to trace, with the oil, the sign of the cross on the forehead of the newly baptized.[20] The minister's thumb traces the sign, with the hand resting on the candidate's forehead. As the sign is made, the minister says: "_____, child of the covenant, you have been sealed." On page 39 of this resource, an alternate text is provided.[21]

Whether or not there is laying on of hands or anointing with oil, the prayer for the gift of the Holy Spirit and the declaration that follows are used, because the meaning applies whether or not the actions accompany the words.

It should be understood that the laying on of hands and anointing with oil are part of a single action and, with the prayer and the washing, express the fullness of the biblical teaching about baptism.

Welcome

As those baptized are welcomed, it is declared that the new Christians are "members of the household of God." They are not alone, left to their own resources to live as Christians. In baptism, the congregation therefore assumes a responsibility to nurture the new Christians and is admonished "to nurture and to love them, and to assist them to be faithful disciples." The congregation, in accepting its responsibility, welcomes the newly baptized "with joy and thanksgiving." Since baptism is not a private affair but is entrance into the family of God, the church of Jesus Christ, it is fitting that our relationship with Christ be expressed with the sharing of signs of peace as the concluding act of baptism.

It is highly appropriate to follow baptism with a celebration of the Lord's Supper. The Proposed Chapter suggests this in its concluding words: "The congregation's welcome shall be extended, God's peace may be exchanged, and the Table may be set."[22]

When the two sacraments are celebrated in the same service, their intimate relationship is emphasized, for through baptism the church is created and in the Supper the church is sustained. From ancient times, Christian initiation culminated with the new Christians joining the congregation at the holy Table. Thus Christian initiation has traditionally included three actions: washing with water, anointing with oil, and celebration of the Eucharist.[23]

Intercession

Prayers for those baptized, parents, and sponsors should be included in the prayers of intercession of the service in which the baptism occurs. The resource provides prayers that may be used. The prayer of blessing in the baptismal rite is a powerful prayer of intercession for the one being baptized. Other prayers at that point could detract from that act of blessing. Rather than additional intercessions being included in the baptismal liturgy itself, their inclusion in the prayers of intercession will make the baptism integral to the service. Texts for such prayers are provided on pages 42–43.

Baptismal Space

The three liturgical centers for Christian worship are font, pulpit, and table. These three centers accommodate the actions of Christian worship: baptism, reading and interpretation of the scripture, and the Lord's Supper.[24] The pulpit has long dominated Protestant worship space. During this century, influenced by the Liturgical Movement, the table has increasingly come to prominence along with the pulpit. However, the space for baptism is only now beginning to be taken seriously.

The fact that baptismal space is minimal reflects the lack of attention the church has given to baptism. Too often, no recognized space is provided; instead, a small bowl is brought out and used when there is a baptism. Even when a font is provided, it often has no place of prominence. The result is that many church buildings provide little or no evidence that Christians baptize. If baptism is to have the centrality in Christian worship that belongs to it, along with Word and Holy Communion, careful attention needs to be given to the space for this sacrament.

The location of the space for baptism is important and can convey significant sacramental meaning. The commentary on the Proposed Chapter suggests four possibilities for locating the baptismal pool or font: "Locating it at the entrance to the worship space calls attention to baptism as initiation into the community of faith and reminds those who pass it of their own baptism. Placed at the center of the worship space it emphasizes the centrality of baptism to our common life in Christ. When situated near the pulpit or lectern, the link between baptism and the Word is made evident. When situated near the Table, the relationship of the sacraments is attested."[25]

The space surrounding the font or pool should be uncrowded so the importance of baptism may be symbolized without distraction or competition from either the pulpit or communion table. Ample space about the font or pool also provides room for at least a portion of the congregation to gather together at the water when a baptism is celebrated.

In some recently built churches, a baptismal pool with recirculating water is located in the back of the sanctuary, between the major entrance and the pews. The continually flowing water has life. It can be seen and heard by the worshipers. Such a provision for baptism gives strong focus to the importance and centrality of baptism in Christian worship.

The advantage of a pool is that it is of sufficient size to signify the importance of the sacrament and stands prominently as a reminder of the living water of baptism. Some of the pools are large enough for immersion, although all enable water to be used in abundance in baptism. Whether a church has a pool or a font, it should be designed to accommodate the use of a generous amount of water in baptism. Water should dominate both in the space for baptism and in the baptismal action itself.[26]

Other Actions

The Reformed tradition long resisted what it considered extraneous things, lest the centrality of water in baptism be weakened and the people confused as to what baptism is. It was frequently insisted that baptism was to be with water alone, with no other ceremony added.

Baptism with water in the name of the triune God is all that is required of a valid sacrament, but adding other signs from the church's baptismal tradition can enrich and give deep meaning to the baptismal event. We need to keep in mind the sixteenth-century ecclesiastical situation that caused the Reformers' violent reactions. We live in times that are very different. Unlike the Reformers, we are called to witness in the context of secularism, where sterile rituals leave us spiritually malnourished. Recovery of those signs from our broader Christian heritage that are rich with theological significance can mark the presence of God in our day and link us with the faith tradition of the centuries. Such worship will once again unite our bodies with our minds.[27]

A caution is nevertheless still in order, which is implicit in a Proposed Chapter statement made in relation to adding other ceremony: "Care shall be taken that the central act of baptizing with water is not overshadowed."[28] Before other signs are added to baptismal practice, water needs to be used in baptism more abundantly than is often the case. But when water is used more generously and dramatically, there is little danger of obscuring the centrality of water in baptism when the actions long associated with baptism are added.

In addition to water, the major traditional ritual acts which have been a part of baptism are the laying on of hands and the anointing with oil, marking with the sign of the cross. Other signs have also been and continue to be a meaningful part of the celebration of baptism.

Of these other signs, perhaps the most useful is the giving of a candle to the newly baptized. Since ancient times the candle given the candidate has been lighted from the paschal candle of the Easter vigil. It is given as a sign of the light which comes from the risen Christ, and it expresses the link between every baptism and Christ's death and resurrection. It further signifies the life the baptized are to live.

In order that the significance of the action not be distorted, it is important that candles be given to the baptized only if the paschal candle is a part of the Easter tradition of the congregation. We are the light of the world only as we are in relation to Christ who is the

Light of the World. The meaning of the action is obscured if candles are given to the newly baptized where there is no symbolic representation of the risen Christ who is the Light of the World. Nevertheless, in congregations where a paschal candle is used, the action can emphasize an important aspect of the meaning of baptism and direct the new Christian toward the life the baptized are to live.

The paschal candle is a sign of the death and resurrection of Jesus Christ and is central to the Easter vigil. It then remains near the communion table through the Easter season.[29] It is lighted each Sunday from Easter through Pentecost Sunday. After Pentecost Sunday, it is placed beside the baptismal font and lighted only on occasions of a baptism. When candles are given to the newly baptized at their baptism, they are lighted from the paschal candle and then given to the newly baptized or parent(s). If a sponsor is a part of the baptismal celebration, the sponsor may be invited to receive the unlighted candle from the hands of the minister. The sponsor then lights the candle from the paschal candle and gives it to the newly baptized or parent(s). As the candle is given, the minister or sponsor may say one of the following:

Let your light so shine before others
that they may see your good works
and glorify your Father in heaven.   *Matt. 5:16*

Christ has given you light.
Walk as children of the light,
and keep the flame of faith burning in your heart.

You have passed from darkness to light.
Shine as a light in the world to the glory of God.

A candle given in baptism can be particularly useful in helping persons "remember" their baptism. The candle may be lighted on the anniversary of baptism, as part of a family's worship. The story of Jesus' baptism (Matt. 3:13–17; Mark 1:4–11; or Luke 3:15–17, 21–22) may be read, prayers may be said, and gifts having spiritual significance may be given. Parents can describe the occasion of the child's baptism. It is a growing practice for church school teachers to send greetings to their pupils on anniversaries of baptism. The occasion of birth into the family of God is thereby marked, rather than their physical birth. In ways such as these, children can "remember" their baptism as an important event in their life, `ust as they "remember" their physical birth on each birthday. Even for adults, such a marking of the anniversary of baptism can reinforce the importance of the event and remind us that as Christians we live out of our baptism.

Baptism is at the center of our lives as Christians. It is important in our living in Christ for as long as we live. Marking our birth as Christians, baptism is the sign of the grace of God, of the covenant God has established with us, of our participation in the death and resurrection with Christ, of our cleansing from sin, and of the presence of the Holy Spirit working among us to comfort, strengthen, and empower us in God's service. As such, baptism should contribute to our spiritual growth and direct us in serving God. When the church baptizes persons in ways that evidence the centrality and importance of baptism in the Christian life, baptism will more effectively point us to God, who is the source of strength and comfort for all of life until our baptism is made complete in death.

THE RENEWAL
OF BAPTISM

AFFIRMING GOD'S GIFT
IN BAPTISM

Very early in the history of the church in the West, as early as the late second century, a tension developed concerning the significance of baptism for the forgiveness of sins and the fact that those who were baptized were still sinful. Various ways emerged to deal with this tension.

One way was to define sin in such a manner that most Christians could avoid committing sins. Sin was seen as acts only: specific incidents of murder, adultery, theft, and so forth. But there were two major weaknesses in this view. First, some Christians did commit such acts. Second, sins such as hatred, lust, covetousness that did not lead to specific acts of murder, adultery, and theft tended not to be thought of as sin. Yet these are the forms of sin that pervade our lives. Occasionally, groups of Christians would object to the church's forgiveness of such acts of sin on the part of those who had repented and go off to form their own community of true "sinless" Christians, claiming that they were the only true church.

Another approach used by Christians was the postponement of baptism for as long as possible. They were well aware that sin was far broader than specific acts and that even well-intentioned Christians occasionally were tempted to commit such acts. They also opposed the baptism of infants. As they saw matters, the problem was not that baptism of infants was invalid but rather that it was quite valid, and therefore the one possibility for the forgiveness of sins had been given to an infant, and it was impossible to imagine that child growing into full maturity as a Christian without committing a sin. So baptism on a deathbed became their ideal. But the major part of the church had difficulty with this opinion, too, and continued to struggle with the tension between baptism for the forgiveness of sins given only once and the continuing power of sin even in the lives of Christians.

Yet another solution to the tension was found in creating an additional sacrament to deal with sins after baptism. This was called "penance," in English usually referred to as "confession." Baptism was understood to remove the guilt of all sin up to the point of baptism, even original sin, a sinful human condition even infants possessed. Penance dealt with the guilt of sins committed by responsible persons after baptism and restored them to their baptismal purity. The exact age at which a child became responsible was not always clear and varied over the centuries. However, a new stage in the Christian life was begun with a child's first confession. This was the understanding that existed at the time of the Protestant Reformation in the sixteenth century.

Martin Luther struggled with the issue. Forgiveness of sins and our need for a sign of assurance that God had indeed forgiven us were extremely important to him. Penance had been a significant sacrament in his life as a monk. Finally he decided that baptism was the sacrament of forgiveness, and that whatever significance had been given to penance had been taken away from baptism. Baptism not only covered sins committed before baptism, it was also an effective sign of God's forgiveness of sins after baptism, when the promises of God were clung to by faith. Faith, a living, life-transforming confidence in God, was the means by which the promises given in baptism became effective in the present, even years after that original baptism. Such faith clearly involved repentance and the desire to live according to the will of God. Though he eliminated penance as a sacrament, Luther in no way lost the sense of the power of sin even in the lives of Christians.

John Calvin agreed with Luther that the power of baptism was to be renewed by faith. This continues to be the position of the Reformed tradition.

Other Protestants in the sixteenth century, in groups generally called "Anabaptist," made different decisions. Some returned to theological positions attempted in the early church, with the important difference that they contended that baptism of infants was invalid. They postponed baptism to adulthood and administered it only to those who intended to live life according to the will of God. They also generally interpreted sin as specific acts that could be avoided. Many believed that the church should not countenance sinners, and the process of restoration to membership of those who had sinned was difficult.

In the United States, religious groups generally termed Baptists have some connection with these sixteenth-century Anabaptists, though they also have some roots in the Calvinist wing of the Reformation. For them, baptism is reserved for those who are able to repent and make a profession of faith. There is a hesitancy to claim that baptism accomplishes something; rather, they believe that it signifies a change that has occurred in the individual.

Presbyterians have been influenced by some of these views. Because of this, issues concerning the meaning of baptism and its significance for the lives of Christians continue to be areas of great confusion for many.

In regard to this confusion, Presbyterians have consistently confessed two fundamental convictions with respect to baptism. First, baptism calls us to lead a life of commitment to God's will, a life of Christian discipleship. Second, regardless of when we are baptized, our life as Christians after baptism will never be as totally committed as it should be. We never live up fully to the claim upon us that is part of baptism. Consequently, repentance is an ongoing part of Christian discipleship. Renewal and recommitment are realities that we experience as Christians. It is not surprising therefore that some Presbyterians desire to be "rebaptized" in order to demonstrate this recommitment. But this denies the character of baptism itself, as the sign of God's promise to us and as having a significance for us throughout our lives.

Because baptism does have significance throughout our lives, it is in order, at various times and on various occasions, to acknowledge and to celebrate the grace of God bestowed on us in baptism and to lay claim to that grace. This is what Luther did through his oft-repeated phrase, "I am baptized." Whenever Luther's faith was weakening, or the challenge of evil before him was threatening, he would remember his baptism and find new strength and courage. It is not too much to say that in remembering his baptism Luther experienced again its power and meaning.

To allow the meaning and reality of baptism to pervade all of life is in keeping with the *Westminster Larger Catechism*, which calls for "improving our Baptism" (7.277). Baptism is to be the referent point for our daily lives, with all that it means renewed through daily repentance and faithfulness in discipleship.

Likewise, for centuries, certain communions have encouraged individuals who have been baptized to renew their own baptism when others are baptized. Moreover, renewal of one's baptism is bound up in each celebration of the Eucharist. More recently, certain denominations have provided services for renewal of baptism for use by a congregation. Such services point to a need in our churches today, a need to experience many times the power and grace of our baptism.

Therefore, in addition to the liturgy for baptism, this resource provides several ceremonies for the renewal of baptism. These ceremonies are structured to point to the meaning of baptism as well as to reflect the immediate occasion of recommitment and renewal. In order to show the relation to baptism, they draw on elements of the baptismal rite itself. To make clear the many and varied occasions when renewal of baptism is appropriate, each ceremony is adapted to particular situations that typically occur in the lives of Christians. Six different ceremonies follow: Public Profession of Faith, Renewal of Baptism for Those Who Have Been Estranged from the Church, Renewal of Baptism for a Congregation, Renewal of Baptism Marking Occasions of Growth in Faith, Renewal of Baptism for the Sick and the Dying, and Renewal of Baptism in Pastoral Counseling. In addition, an order for the Reception of Members by Transfer is included.

These services of the renewal of baptism are offered to the church for use by its members. They are implicit in the Proposed Chapter.[30] It is the hope of those who designed the ceremonies that they can help us all experience the ongoing meaning of baptism for our lives, and that God's grace will become more real and more powerful for us as we renew our baptism.

OCCASIONS FOR THE RENEWAL
OF BAPTISM

Public Profession of Faith

This ceremony (p. 73) is for those who have been baptized in infancy and nurtured within the church. This is the ceremony that has traditionally been called "confirmation" or "commissioning." It is an occasion for rejoicing, a time for celebrating growth that has occurred as it should. It is the proper development from baptism, a claiming of the promises and responsibilities that baptism entails. Baptized children are part of the church, yet their response to God's grace leads to new roles within the congregation.[31] In this sense, this particular occasion of the renewal of baptism is a rite of passage from childhood to adulthood within the community of faith. The ceremony needs to include a renewal of the vows of baptism, acknowledgment of the new responsibilities being undertaken, and a prayer of blessing with the laying on of hands for each person.

Renewal of Baptism
for Those Who Have Been Estranged
from the Church

This ceremony (p. 78) is for those baptized who have already made a public profession of faith but who have been estranged from the church. In this situation, the growth from baptism into a mature Christian life has been interrupted for some period of time. There has been a turning away from the community of faith, a lapse in participation. The reasons for this can be many, for which the individual, the church, or both bear the responsibility. But the workings of grace have led to the desire to be again an active part of the people of God. This ceremony needs to involve a renewal of baptismal vows, the acceptance of responsibilities of active membership, and a prayer of blessing with the laying on of hands. A specific welcome into the congregation is also appropriate.

Renewal of Baptism for a Congregation

In the life of every congregation, there are times that call for a public renewal of baptism on the part of the whole congregation (p. 82). Historically, such services of renewal of baptismal vows have been a part of the Easter vigil, held on the Saturday night preceding Easter. Since in baptism we die with Christ and are raised with him to new life, such renewal of vows is an appropriate part of our preparation for the celebration of Easter. There may well be other occasions in the life of a specific congregation when such renewal ceremonies would be appropriate. These services include the renewal of vows as well as a prayer of blessing for the congregation. Such a service is an appropriate preparation for celebrating the Lord's Supper. The gesture of lifting water from the font and making the sign of the cross over the people provides a dramatic reminder of baptism.

Renewal of Baptism
Marking Occasions of Growth in Faith

This ceremony (p. 86) provides for the renewal of baptism by an individual who wishes to mark the occasion of a new sense of commitment, a new level of growth as a Christian, or a sense of calling to a particular ministry, and it can be a public or a private ceremony. It refers to a person who has been a part of the congregation, not estranged from the church, but who has experienced growth in the life of faith that needs to be expressed and celebrated. For some Christians, growth in the life of faith is steady and gradual. For others, plateaus are reached and then new stages dawn with dramatic intensity. There is frequently a desire to mark such occasions with a ceremony of renewal, public or private. There is no change in the person's official relationship to the congregation. The use of a baptismal renewal service shows that this growth is the proper outcome of baptism. A renewal of the vows as well as a prayer of blessing with the laying on of hands is appropriate.

Renewal of Baptism for the Sick and the Dying

The significance of our baptism lasts the whole life, and our death is the fulfillment of the dying with Christ that our baptism promises. Illness, even when it is not life-threatening, is often the occasion for a new sense of our need for Christ's presence with us in our suffering and weakness. Forms of baptismal renewal (p. 92) can therefore be helpful in ministries to the sick and the dying. These may be full renewal of vows with a prayer of blessing and the laying on of hands, or the significance of the vows can be included in the prayer of blessing when it seems more appropriate not to include the responses of the ill person.

Renewal of Baptism in Pastoral Counseling

Since pastoral counseling often deals with the personal struggles to live up to the high calling of our baptism, a private ceremony of renewal may well be appropriate within such a counseling relationship (p. 94). It may include the renewal of the vows as well as a prayer of blessing with the laying on of hands. This is clearly a private rather than a public ceremony.

Reception of Members by Transfer

When new members are added to a local congregation by letter of transfer, the renewal of baptismal vows is not usually appropriate. Such persons need to be asked about their desire to be part of this congregation and they need to be welcomed (p. 96). But any indication that there has been a lapse in their participation in the body of Christ or that this new congregation has questions about the faith of the congregation from which they have moved is destructive of the unity of the church, a central tenet of the Reformed tradition. A ceremony for the reception of new members by transfer is included, but it is not a service of renewal of baptismal vows. It is a joyful welcoming of those who have been and continue to be active participants in the life of the church.

Occasionally, baptized persons who once made a profession of faith and were active members in another church are unable to obtain a certificate of transfer when they wish to join another church. Such persons are asked to reaffirm their faith. One of the following services may be adapted depending upon the circumstances: Public Profession of Faith (p. 73), Renewal of Baptism for Those Who Have Been Estranged from the Church (p. 78), or Renewal of Baptism Marking Occasions of Growth in Faith (p. 86).

It is critical in all these ceremonies, as well as in baptism itself, that baptism does not mark the end of a process but rather its beginning. The whole Christian life is lived out of baptism, and growth is expected. Nor is growth always even and without interruption or regressive periods. The vitality of baptism, based on God's promises to us, is so great, however, that baptism itself does not need to be repeated, as though we ever lost our baptism. But stages of growth, the end of interruptions in our growth as Christians, can and should be appropriately marked by recalling to us and to the whole congregation the meaning of our common baptism. These suggested services are consistent with this understanding.

SERVICES FOR THE RENEWAL
OF BAPTISM

PUBLIC PROFESSION OF FAITH

This service is for persons who were baptized as infants and nurtured in the church, and who now are making a public profession of faith.

PRESENTATION

A hymn, psalm, spiritual, or other suitable music may be sung while those who are making a public profession of faith gather before the congregation.

An ELDER, representing the session, presents the candidates:

_____, _____ *are* presented by the session
for the renewal of *their* baptism.
They have studied God's Word
and *have* learned the belief and practice of the church.
They now *desire* to profess publicly *their* faith,
and assume greater responsibility in the life of the church,
and its mission in the world.

The MINISTER says:

We rejoice that you now desire to declare your faith
and to share with us in our common ministry.
In baptism you were joined to Christ
and made *members* of his church.

In the community of the people of God,
you have learned of God's purpose for you and for all creation.
You have been nurtured at the table of our Lord
and called to witness to the gospel of Jesus Christ.

> *The MINISTER continues, using one or more of the following scriptures:*

Hear these words from Holy Scripture:

You are fellow citizens with the saints
and members of the household of God,
built upon the foundation of the apostles and prophets,
Christ Jesus himself being the cornerstone,
in whom the whole structure is joined together
and grows into a holy temple in the Lord;
in whom you also are built into it
for a dwelling place of God in the Spirit.   *Eph. 2:19–22*

We are God's workmanship,
created in Christ Jesus for good works,
which God prepared beforehand,
that we should walk in them.   *Eph. 2:10*

You are a chosen race, a royal priesthood,
a holy nation, God's own people,
that you may declare the wonderful deeds of God,
who called you out of darkness
into God's marvelous light.   *1 Peter 2:9*

You are the light of the world.
A city set on a hill cannot be hid.
No one lights a lamp and puts it under a bushel,
but on a stand,
and it gives light to all in the house.
Let your light so shine before others,
that they may see your good works
and give glory to your Father who is in heaven.   *Matt. 5:14–16*

RENUNCIATION AND AFFIRMATION

Now, as you publicly declare your faith,
I ask you to reject sin,

to profess your faith in Christ Jesus,
and to confess the faith of the church,
the faith in which you were baptized.

Do you renounce evil,
and its power in the world,
which defies God's righteousness and love?

I renounce them.

Do you renounce the ways of sin
that separate you from the love of God?

I renounce them.

Do you turn to Jesus Christ
and accept him as your Lord and Savior?

I do.

Do you intend to be Christ's faithful disciple,
obeying his word, and showing his love,
to your life's end?

I do.

With the whole church,
let us confess our faith.

> *The CONGREGATION stands and joins the CANDIDATES in affirming the faith in the words of the Apostles' Creed.*

**I believe in God, the Father almighty,
    creator of heaven and earth.**

**I believe in Jesus Christ, his only Son, our Lord.
    He was conceived by the power of the Holy Spirit
        and born of the Virgin Mary.
    He suffered under Pontius Pilate,
        was crucified, died, and was buried.
    He descended to the dead.
    On the third day he rose again.
    He ascended into heaven,
        and is seated at the right hand of the Father.
    He will come again to judge the living and the dead.**

I believe in the Holy Spirit,
   the holy catholic church,
   the communion of saints,
   the forgiveness of sins,
   the resurrection of the body,
   and the life everlasting. Amen.

The MINISTER addresses the candidates making a profession of faith:

You have publicly professed your faith.
Do you intend to continue in the covenant God made with you
   in your baptism,
to be a faithful member of this congregation,
to share in its ministry through your prayers and gifts,
your study and service,
and so fulfill your calling to be a disciple of Jesus Christ?

I do.

Let us pray.

Gracious God, through water and the Spirit
you claimed *these* your *servants* as your own.
You cleansed *them* of *their* sins, gave *them* new life,
and bound *them* to your service.
Renew in *them* the covenant you made in *their* baptism
Send *them* forth in the power of the Spirit
to love and serve you with joy,
and strive for justice and peace in all the earth,
in the name of Jesus Christ our Lord.

Amen.

THE BLESSING (AND ANOINTING)

The CANDIDATES kneel.

The MINISTER in turn lays both hands upon the head of each candidate while offering the following prayer. The sign of the cross may be marked on the forehead of the candidate, using oil prepared for this purpose:

O Lord, uphold _____ by your Holy Spirit.
Daily increase in *(him, her)* your gifts of grace:

the spirit of wisdom and understanding,
the spirit of counsel and might,
the spirit of knowledge and the fear of the Lord,
the spirit of joy in your presence,
both now and forever.

The CANDIDATE answers:

Amen.

Or

Defend, O Lord, your servant _____
with your heavenly grace,
that *(he, she)* may continue yours forever,
and daily increase in your Holy Spirit more and more,
until *(he, she)* comes to your everlasting kingdom.

The CANDIDATE answers:

Amen.

After each candidate has received the laying on of hands, the MINISTER prays:

Ever-living God,
guard *these* your *servants* with your protecting hand,
and let your Holy Spirit be with *them* forever.
Lead *them* to know and obey your Word
that *they* may serve you in this life
and dwell with you in the life to come;
through Jesus Christ our Lord.

Amen.

An appropriate gift may be given to each person. Such gifts might include a cross or a book of prayers.

The MINISTER and ELDER exchange the peace with those who have renewed their baptism. They may exchange the peace with each other and members of the congregation.

The peace of Christ be with you.

And also with you.

RENEWAL OF BAPTISM
FOR THOSE WHO HAVE BEEN ESTRANGED
FROM THE CHURCH

Baptized persons who have lapsed, but who now desire to participate actively in the life of the church, are restored to membership through reaffirmation of their faith.

PRESENTATION

A hymn, psalm, spiritual, or other suitable music may be sung while those who are reaffirming the faith gather before the congregation.

An ELDER, representing the session, presents those reaffirming the faith:

On behalf of the session, I present _____, _____,
who *desire* to reaffirm the faith into which *they were* baptized.
They have renewed *their* commitment to Christ
and *their* participation in the life and work of the church of Christ.

The MINISTER says:

We rejoice in your return to the household of God
to claim again the promises of God
which are yours through your baptism.

Hear these words from Holy Scripture:

By grace you have been saved through faith;
and this is not your own doing,
it is the gift of God.   *Eph. 2:8*

RENUNCIATION AND AFFIRMATION

Now, as you publicly declare your faith,
I ask you to reject sin,
to profess your faith in Christ Jesus,
and to confess the faith of the church,
the faith in which you were baptized.

Do you renounce evil, and its power in the world,
which defies God's righteousness and love?

I renounce them.

Do you renounce the ways of sin
that separate you from the love of God?

I renounce them.

Do you turn to Jesus Christ
and accept him as your Lord and Savior?

I do.

Do you intend to be Christ's faithful disciple,
obeying his word, and showing his love,
to your life's end?

I do.

With the whole church,
let us confess our faith.

> *The CONGREGATION stands and joins THOSE RENEWING THEIR BAPTISM in affirming the faith in the words of the Apostles' Creed.*

I believe in God, the Father almighty,
  creator of heaven and earth.

I believe in Jesus Christ, his only Son, our Lord.
  He was conceived by the power of the Holy Spirit
    and born of the Virgin Mary.
  He suffered under Pontius Pilate,
    was crucified, died, and was buried.
  He descended to the dead.
  On the third day he rose again.
  He ascended into heaven,
    and is seated at the right hand of the Father.
  He will come again to judge the living and the dead.

I believe in the Holy Spirit,
  the holy catholic church,
  the communion of saints,
  the forgiveness of sins,
  the resurrection of the body,
  and the life everlasting. Amen.

The MINISTER addresses those renewing their baptism:

You have publicly professed your faith.
Do you intend to continue in the covenant God made with you
   in your baptism,
to be a faithful member of this congregation,
to share in its ministry through your prayers and gifts,
your study and service,
and so fulfill your calling to be a disciple of Jesus Christ?

I do.

Let us pray.

Faithful God,
you work in us and for us
even when we do not know it.
You call us back to yourself
when we follow on a different path.
We thank you for restoring, to the fellowship of your people,
your *servants* _____, _____.
Renew in *them* the covenant you made in *their* baptism.
By the power of your Spirit,
strengthen *them* in faith and love,
that *they* may serve you with joy,
to the glory of Jesus Christ our Lord.

Amen.

THE BLESSING (AND ANOINTING)

The CANDIDATES kneel.

*The MINISTER in turn lays both hands upon the head of each
candidate while offering the following prayer. The sign of the cross
may be marked on the forehead of the candidate, using oil prepared
for this purpose:*

O Lord, uphold _____ by your Holy Spirit.
Daily increase in *(him, her)* your gifts of grace:
the spirit of wisdom and understanding,
the spirit of counsel and might,
the spirit of knowledge and the fear of the Lord,

the spirit of joy in your presence,
both now and forever.

The CANDIDATE answers:

Amen.

Or

Defend, O Lord, your servant _____
with your heavenly grace,
that *(he, she)* may continue yours forever,
and daily increase in your Holy Spirit more and more,
until *(he, she)* comes to your everlasting kingdom.

The CANDIDATE answers:

Amen.

*After each candidate has received the laying on of hands, the
MINISTER prays:*

Ever-living God,
guard *these* your *servants* with your protecting hand,
and let your Holy Spirit be with *them* forever.
Lead *them* to know and obey your Word
that *they* may serve you in this life
and dwell with you in the life to come;
through Jesus Christ our Lord.

Amen.

*The MINISTER and ELDER representing the session welcome the
members in an appropriate manner using these or similar words.*

Welcome to this congregation and its ministry.
The peace of Christ be with you.

And also with you.

*The MINISTER and ELDER exchange the peace with those who have
renewed their baptism. They may exchange the peace with each other
and members of the congregation.*

RENEWAL OF BAPTISM
FOR A CONGREGATION

It is appropriate that this service be led by the MINISTER from the baptismal font or pool, which should be filled with water.

After the sermon has been preached, the MINISTER, using one or more of the following scriptures, says:

Hear these words from Holy Scripture:

Know therefore that the Lord your God is God,
the faithful God who keeps covenant and steadfast love
with those who love God
and keep God's commandments.   *Deut. 7:9*

God has showed you what is good;
and what does the Lord require of you
but to do justice, and to love kindness,
and to walk humbly with your God?   *Micah 6:8*

Once you were darkness,
but now you are light in the Lord;
walk as children of light . . .
and try to learn what is pleasing to the Lord.   *Eph. 5:8, 10*

Lead a life worthy of the calling to which you have been called,
with all lowliness and meekness,
with patience, forbearing one another in love,
eager to maintain the unity of the Spirit
in the bond of peace.   *Eph. 4:1–3*

The CONGREGATION stands, as the MINISTER continues:

Sisters and brothers in Christ,
our baptism is the sign and seal
of our cleansing from sin,
and of our being grafted into Christ.
Through the birth, life, death, and resurrection of Christ,
the power of sin was broken
and God's kingdom entered our world.

Through our baptism we were made citizens of that kingdom,
and freed from the bondage of sin.
Let us celebrate that freedom and redemption
through the renewal of our baptism.

RENUNCIATION AND AFFIRMATION

I ask you, therefore,
once again to reject sin,
to profess your faith in Christ Jesus,
and to confess the faith of the church,
the faith in which we were baptized.

Do you renounce evil,
and its power in the world,
which defies God's righteousness and love?

I renounce them.

Do you renounce the ways of sin
that separate you from the love of God?

I renounce them.

Do you turn to Jesus Christ
and accept him as your Lord and Savior?

I do.

Do you intend to be Christ's faithful disciple,
obeying his word, and showing his love,
to your life's end?

I do.

With the whole church,
let us confess our faith.

> *The CONGREGATION affirms the faith in the words of the Apostles'
> Creed.*

**I believe in God, the Father almighty,
    creator of heaven and earth.**

I believe in Jesus Christ, his only Son, our Lord.
> **He was conceived by the power of the Holy Spirit**
> > **and born of the Virgin Mary.**
> **He suffered under Pontius Pilate,**
> > **was crucified, died, and was buried.**
> **He descended to the dead.**
> **On the third day he rose again.**
> **He ascended into heaven,**
> > **and is seated at the right hand of the Father.**
> **He will come again to judge the living and the dead.**

I believe in the Holy Spirit,
> **the holy catholic church,**
> **the communion of saints,**
> **the forgiveness of sins,**
> **the resurrection of the body,**
> **and the life everlasting. Amen.**

> *The MINISTER leads the people in prayer, saying:*

Let us pray.

God of life and goodness,
we praise you for claiming us through our baptism
and for upholding us by your grace.
We remember your promises given to us in our baptism.
Strengthen us by your Spirit,
that we may obey your will
and serve you with joy;
through Jesus Christ our Lord.

Amen.

> *The MINISTER may place his or her hand into the water of the font,
> lift up some water, let it fall back into the font, and then make the
> sign of the cross over the people, while saying:*

Remember your baptism and be thankful.

In the name of the Father and of the Son and of the Holy Spirit.

Amen.

The MINISTER may invite persons who wish to receive the laying on of hands to come and kneel at the font. The sign of the cross may be traced upon the forehead of each person and may include the anointing with oil. Laying both hands upon the head of each person in turn, the MINISTER says:

O Lord, uphold _____ by your Holy Spirit.
Daily increase in *(him, her)* your gifts of grace:
the spirit of wisdom and understanding,
the spirit of counsel and might,
the spirit of knowledge and the fear of the Lord,
the spirit of joy in your presence,
both now and forever.

> *The CANDIDATE answers:*

Amen.

> *Or*

Defend, O Lord, your servant _____
with your heavenly grace,
that *(he, she)* may continue yours forever,
and daily increase in your Holy Spirit more and more,
until *(he, she)* comes to your everlasting kingdom.

> *The CANDIDATE answers:*

Amen.

> *The service concludes with the exchange of peace.*

The peace of Christ be with you.
And also with you.

> *A celebration of the Lord's Supper may follow.*

RENEWAL OF BAPTISM
MARKING OCCASIONS OF GROWTH IN FAITH

This service may be used in a variety of situations, such as when an individual experiences a significant deepening of commitment or answers the call to a particular ministry in the church. The service may be either private or in the context of corporate worship.

The MINISTER may read one or more of the following, or other appropriate scripture:

Remember the words of Jesus:

You shall love the Lord your God
with all your heart,
and with all your soul,
and with all your mind.
This is the great and first commandment.
And a second is like it,
You shall love your neighbor as yourself.
On these two commandments
depend all the law and the prophets.   *Matt. 22:37–40*

Then the King will say to those at his right hand,
"Come, O blessed of my Father,
inherit the kingdom prepared for you
from the foundation of the world;
for I was hungry and you gave me food,
I was thirsty and you gave me drink,
I was a stranger and you welcomed me,
I was naked and you clothed me,
I was sick and you visited me,
I was in prison and you came to me."   *Matt. 25:34–36*

The harvest is plentiful,
but the laborers are few;
pray therefore the Lord of the harvest
to send out laborers into his harvest.   *Luke 10:2*

I am the light of the world;
those who follow me will not walk in darkness,
but will have the light of life.   *John 8:12*

For what will it profit a person,
if the whole world is gained
and life is forfeited?   *Matt. 16:26*

No longer do I call you servants,
for servants do not know what their master is doing;
but I have called you friends,
for all that I have heard from my Father
I have made known to you.
You did not choose me,
but I chose you and appointed you
that you should go and bear fruit
and that your fruit should abide;
so that the Father may give to you
whatever you ask in my name.   *Iohn 15:15–16*

Scripture also instructs us:

Serve the Lord with gladness;
come before God with shouts of joy.
Know that the Lord is God!
We belong to the One who made us,
to God, who tends us like sheep.
The Lord is good;
and will love us forever.
God is faithful from age to age.   *Ps. 100:2–3, 5*

I appeal to you, by the mercies of God,
to present your bodies as a living sacrifice,
holy and acceptable to God,
which is your spiritual worship.   *Rom. 12:1*

Whatever you do, in word or deed,
do everything in the name of the Lord Jesus,
giving thanks to God through him.   *Col. 3:17*

God is at work in you,
both to will and to work for God's good pleasure   *Phil. 2:13*

The MINISTER continues:

The call of Christ is to willing, dedicated discipleship.
Our discipleship is a manifestation of the new life
into which we enter through baptism.
It is possible because in Jesus Christ
we have been set free from the bondage of sin and death.
Discipleship is both a gift and a commitment,
an offering and a responsibility.
It is marked by change, growth, and deepened commitment.
 t is lived out of a renewing sense of God's calling to us,
and of God's claim upon us made in our baptism.

On this occasion we celebrate with _____, _____,
and join with *them*
in renewing *their* baptism.

> *Here the MINISTER may tell what has happened in each individual's life, or the PERSON(S) renewing their baptism may share relevant information.*

> *The MINISTER says:*

The grace bestowed on you in baptism
is sufficient because it is God's grace.
By God's grace we are saved,
and enabled to grow in the faith,
and to commit our lives in ways which please God.

I invite you now to claim that grace given you in baptism
by renewing your baptismal vows,
to renounce all that opposes God and God's kingdom
and to affirm the faith of the holy catholic church.

> *The MINISTER continues, using the following renunciations and affirmations or some appropriate alternatives.*

Do you renounce evil,
and its power in the world,
which defies God's righteousness and love?

I renounce them.

Do you renounce the ways of sin
that separate you from the love of God?

I renounce them.

Do you turn to Jesus Christ
and accept him as your Lord and Savior?

I do.

Do you intend to be Christ's faithful disciple,
obeying his word, and showing his love,
to your life's end?

I do.

With the whole church,
let us confess our faith.

> *THOSE PRESENT stand up and join THE INDIVIDUAL(S) in affirming the faith in the words of the Apostles' Creed.*

I believe in God, the Father almighty,
  creator of heaven and earth.

I believe in Jesus Christ, his only Son, our Lord.
  He was conceived by the power of the Holy Spirit
    and born of the Virgin Mary.
  He suffered under Pontius Pilate,
    was crucified, died, and was buried.
  He descended to the dead.
  On the third day he rose again.
  He ascended into heaven,
    and is seated at the right hand of the Father.
  He will come again to judge the living and the dead.

I believe in the Holy Spirit,
  the holy catholic church,
  the communion of saints,
  the forgiveness of sins,
  the resurrection of the body,
  and the life everlasting. Amen.

The MINISTER and the PEOPLE pray together:

Let us pray.

O God, we rejoice in your grace, given and received.
We thank you that you claim us
and are working in our lives
to strengthen, encourage, and guide us.
We praise you
for opportunities to serve in your kingdom,
and for your Spirit,
empowering us to live a life worthy of our calling.
Root and establish us in love,
that, with all God's people, we may have power
to comprehend the deep meaning of our life in Christ.
Strengthen us in faith
that we may know the love of Christ,
even though it is beyond knowledge,
and so be filled with all the fullness of God;
through Jesus Christ our Lord. Amen.

THE BLESSING (AND ANOINTING)

The MINISTER may lay hands on the head of the person(s) while saying:

O Lord, uphold _____ by your Holy Spirit.
Daily increase in *(him, her)* your gifts of grace:
the spirit of wisdom and understanding,
the spirit of counsel and might,
the spirit of knowledge and the fear of the Lord,
the spirit of joy in your presence,
both now and forever.

The CANDIDATES answer:

Amen.

The MINISTER here may mark the sign of the cross on the forehead of each person, using oil prepared for this purpose, saying these or similar words:

_____, you are a disciple of Jesus Christ.
Walk in love, as Christ loved us
and gave himself for us.
Rejoice always, pray constantly,
give thanks in all circumstances;
for this is the will of God in Christ Jesus for you.

THE PEACE

The MINISTER says these or similar words:

The peace of God, which passes all understanding,
keep your heart and your mind in Christ Jesus.   *Phil. 4:7*

Amen.

If this renewal of baptism is part of a public service, all may exchange signs of peace.

RENEWAL OF BAPTISM
FOR THE SICK AND THE DYING

This ceremony may take place at the bedside of the sick or dying person. Normally the minister will be accompanied by one or more elders.

The ceremony may also be used in special services for those members of the congregation who seek wholeness and who come together for the purpose of renewing their baptism in the midst of illness.

One or more of the following scriptures may be read: Psalms 23; 46:1–7; 90; 91; Luke 17:11–19; 2 Corinthians 1:3–5; Philippians 4:4–7.

Using these or similar words, the MINISTER says:

Through baptism you were joined to Christ,
in his death and resurrection,
and entered the covenant God has established.
In this covenant, the grace of God sustains and nourishes us
and strengthens our faith in the gift of life eternal,
which is ours in Christ.
Christ himself is our comfort and hope in illness
It is he who brings us to wholeness of life.

The MINISTER continues, having determined whether all or any portions of the following renunciations and affirmations are appropriate in the situation.

I ask you, therefore, once again to reject sin,
to profess your faith in Christ Jesus,
and to confess the faith of the church,
the faith in which we are baptized.

Do you renounce evil, and its power in the world,
which defies God's righteousness and love?

I renounce them.

Do you renounce the ways of sin
that separate you from the love of God?

I renounce them.

Do you turn to Jesus Christ
and accept him as your Lord and Savior?

I do.

Do you intend to be Christ's faithful disciple,
obeying his word, and showing his love, to your life's end?

I do.

Let us pray.

> *The MINISTER offers a prayer that is relevant to the particular*
> *person(s) being ministered to. It may include thanksgiving, petition,*
> *intercession, confession, and forgiveness.*
>
> *The MINISTER, laying hands upon each person who is sick or dying,*
> *offers the following prayer. The sign of the cross may be marked on*
> *the forehead of each person being ministered to, using oil prepared for*
> *this purpose:*

Defend, O Lord, your servant _____
with your heavenly grace,
that *(he, she)* may continue yours forever,
and daily increase in your Holy Spirit more and more,
until *(he, she)* comes to your everlasting kingdom.

Amen.

> *After each person has received the laying on of hands, the MINISTER*
> *prays this or another appropriate prayer:*

Ever-living God, guard your *servants* _____, _____
with your protecting hand
and let your Holy Spirit be with *them* forever.
Lead *them* to know and obey your Word
that *they* may serve you in this life
and dwell with you in the life to come;
through Jesus Christ our Lord.

Amen.

The peace of Christ be with you.

Amen.

> *Holy Communion may be celebrated.*

RENEWAL OF BAPTISM
IN PASTORAL COUNSELING

This is a private ceremony for use in pastoral counseling with persons who struggle to live up to the implications of their baptism.

One or more of the following scriptures may be read:

Psalm 23   2 Corinthians 1:3–5
Psalm 90   Philippians 4:4–7
Psalm 91

Using these or similar words, the MINISTER says:

In your baptism, God acted out of grace and love for you.
You entered the covenant God established.
You were joined to Christ
and welcomed into the household of faith.
The grace of God is eternal.
Nothing can separate you from God's love.
You are still God's child,
and God cares for you.

The MINISTER continues:

I ask you, therefore,
once again to reject sin,
to profess your faith in Christ Jesus,
and to confess the faith of the church,
the faith in which we are baptized.

Do you renounce evil,
and its power in the world,
which defies God's righteousness and love?

I renounce them.

Do you renounce the ways of sin
that separate you from the love of God?

I renounce them.

Do you turn to Jesus Christ
and accept him as your Lord and Savior?

I do.

Do you intend to be Christ's faithful disciple,
obeying his word, and showing his love,
to your life's end?

I do.

Let us pray.

> *The MINISTER offers a prayer that is relevant to the particular concerns that have been part of the counseling situation. It may include thanksgiving, petition, intercession, confession, and forgiveness.*
>
> *The MINISTER continues with the laying on of hands:*

Defend, O Lord, your servant _____
with your heavenly grace,
that *(he, she)* may continue yours forever,
and daily increase in your Holy Spirit more and more,
until *(he, she)* comes to your everlasting kingdom.

Amen.

The peace of Christ be with you.

Amen.

RECEPTION OF MEMBERS
BY TRANSFER

An ELDER representing the session shall name those who have been received by transfer from other Christian churches, saying:

_____, _____ *have* been received into the membership of this congregation by transfer from _____ congregation.

THOSE TO BE RECEIVED present themselves before the congregation.

The MINISTER says:

There is one body and one Spirit,
just as you were called to the one hope
that belongs to your call,
one Lord, one faith, one baptism,
one God and Father of us all,
who is above all and through all and in all.   *Eph. 4:4–6*

You come to us as members of the one holy catholic church,
into which you were baptized,
and by which you have been nurtured.
We now welcome you to the worship and work of this congregation.
We are one with each other,
brothers and sisters in the Lord.
We rejoice in the gifts you bring to us.

Do you promise to be a faithful member of this congregation,
to share in its ministry
through your prayers and your gifts,
your study and your service,
and so fulfill your calling
to be a disciple of Jesus Christ?

I do.

Let the ELDER representing the session lead the people in prayer, saying:

Let us pray.

Holy God, we praise you for calling us to be a servant people,
and for gathering us into the body of Christ.
We thank you for choosing to add to our number
brothers and sisters in faith.
Together, may we live in your Spirit,
and so love one another,
that we may have the mind of Jesus Christ our Lord,
to whom we give honor and glory forever.
Amen.

Let the MINISTER and ELDER representing the session welcome the new members in an appropriate manner, using these or similar words.

Welcome to this congregation and its ministry.

Peace be with you.

And also with you.

It is appropriate for the congregation to share signs of peace as the new members return to their places.

ADAPTING THE SERVICES FOR PARTICULAR CIRCUMSTANCES

In order to preserve the integrity of the sacrament, it is preferable that baptism be done separately from services for the renewal of baptism. However, there are situations when this is not advisable. When such situations occur, the minister will need to make appropriate adaptations, combining elements of the two services in order to avoid the needless repeating of the renunciations and the Apostles' Creed. The adaptations will vary according to the particular situation.

An example of such adaptation will illustrate what is required. A young family indicates a desire to unite with the congregation. The woman was confirmed in another denomination but became inactive and is unable to obtain a certificate of transfer. The husband was baptized as an infant but never has made a profession of faith. They are presenting their baby for baptism. In this situation, there is a reaffirmation of faith, a profession of faith, and a baptism. It is appropriate that this be done in a single service. The services may be adapted for these particular circumstances as follows:

PRESENTATION

The MINISTER reads verses of scripture from those provided (pp. 25–26), beginning with Matthew 28:18–20.

An ELDER, representing the session, presents the candidates, using the sentences provided for the presentation in each of the services (pp. 26, 73, 78). In presenting the candidates, the ELDER says:

On behalf of the session:

I present _____ for the renewal of his baptism.
He has studied God's Word
and has learned the belief and practice of the church.
He now desires to profess publicly his faith,
and assume greater responsibility in the life of the church,
and its mission in the world.

I present _____,
who desires to reaffirm the faith into which she was baptized.
She has renewed her commitment to Christ
and her participation in the life and work of the church of Christ.

I present _____ to receive the sacrament of baptism.

The MINISTER says:

We rejoice that you now desire to declare your faith
and to share with us in our common ministry.
In baptism you were joined to Christ
and made a member of his church.
In the community of the people of God,
you have learned of God's purpose for you and for all creation.
You have been nurtured at the table of our Lord,
and called to witness to the gospel of Jesus Christ.

In coming to profess the faith into which you were baptized
do you desire that _____ be baptized?

I do.

Relying on God's grace,
do you promise to live the Christian faith,
and to teach that faith to your child?

I do.

And

The MINISTER addresses the SPONSORS, if any are present:

Do you promise, through prayer and example,
to support and encourage _____
to be a faithful Christian?

I do.

RENUNCIATION AND AFFIRMATION

Through baptism we enter the covenant God has established.
Within that covenant we are given new life
and are guarded from evil,
nurtured by the love of God and God's people.
On our part, we are to turn from evil
and turn to Jesus Christ.

I ask you, therefore,
to reject sin,
to profess your faith in Christ Jesus,
and to confess the faith of the church,
the faith in which you were baptized,
and in which now we baptize _____.

Do you renounce evil . . . ?

The liturgy continues from p. 28 through the Apostles' Creed (p. 29).

The liturgy Public Profession of Faith is then used with the woman and the man, beginning with the minister's words to the candidate following the Apostles' Creed (p. 76): "You have publicly professed. . . ." The prayer that follows may be the prayer on page 76, the prayer on page 80, or an adaptation of the two. The liturgy continues through the prayer, following the laying on of hands (p. 77).

The baptism then proceeds beginning at page 29. The service concludes with the giving of the peace.

For other situations, adaptations may be made in a similar manner depending upon the particular circumstances.

NOTES

1. See note 17.

2. The question in this rite is based on the concluding portion of a long exhortation in Calvin's rite. It reads: "We receive twofold grace and benefit from our God in baptism, provided that we do not destroy the force of this sacrament by our ingratitude. That is, we have in it sure testimony that God wishes to be a merciful Father to us, not imputing to us all our faults and offences: secondly that he will assist us by his Holy Spirit, so that we can do battle against the devil, sin, and the desires of our flesh, until we have victory over them, so as to live in the liberty of his kingdom, which is the kingdom of righteousness." The parents of a child being baptized are asked to make certain promises to nurture their child in the Christian faith, ending with the words: "Also you will exhort him to live according to the rule which our Lord has set forth for us in his law, which briefly consists in these two points, that we love God with all our mind, our heart and strength, and our neighbor as ourselves. Likewise, according to the exhortations which he has given by his prophets and apostles, that renouncing himself and his own desires, he may devote himself and consecrate himself to glorify the name of God and of Jesus Christ and to edify his neighbours." The promises having been made, the name is given to the child, and then the minister baptizes the candidate. (John D. C. Fischer, *Christian Initiation: The Reformation Period*, pp. 114, 116, quoting from the baptismal rite contained in Calvin's *The Form of Prayers and Ecclesiastical Chants with the Manner of Administering the Sacraments and Solemnizing Marriage According to the Custom of the Ancient Church, 1542*.)

3. The "Proposed Chapter on Baptism for a New Directory for Worship and Commentary" (commentary prepared by John F. Jansen) may be ordered from the Advisory Council on Discipleship and Worship, Room 1020, 475 Riverside Drive, New York, NY 10115.

4. Proposed Chapter, 30.211.

5. For further elaboration see Harold M. Daniels, "Baptism," in Harold M. Daniels, ed., *Worship in the Community of Faith*, pp. 89–90.

6. See pages 44–47 for specific suggestions.

7. Proposed Chapter, 30.206.

8. Ibid., 30.214.

9. For an exposition of the use of water in baptism in the Bible and throughout history, the divorce of word and action in baptismal liturgies, and the need to recover the generous use of water in baptism, see John E. Burkhart, "Have All the Seas Gone Dry?" (The full reference for this source, and others similarly cited, appears in the section For Further Reading.)

10. Proposed Chapter, 30.216.

11. Daniels, op. cit., p. 82.

12. Proposed Chapter, 30.218.

13. Daniels, op. cit., pp. 83–84.

14. John F. Jansen, in his commentary on the Proposed Chapter (pp. 26–27), describes the biblical images implicit in each mode: "Each of these modes of baptism expresses biblical imagery. *Pouring* calls to mind the imagery of Joel 2:28 (appropriated in Acts 2:18, 33) of the pouring out of the Holy Spirit. This imagery is explicitly linked with baptism in Titus 3:5, 'by the washing of regeneration and renewal in the Holy Spirit, which he poured out upon us richly through Jesus Christ our Savior.' *Sprinkling* calls to mind the prophetic promise that God 'will sprinkle clean water upon you and make you clean' (Ezek. 36:25), an imagery which the New Testament links with the sprinkled blood of Christ in baptismal allusions (e.g. I Pet. 1:2), more explicitly in Hebrews 10:22, 'with our hearts sprinkled clean from an evil conscience and our bodies washed with pure water.' *Immersion* not only is suggested by such narratives as the baptism of Jesus (Mark 1:10 and parallels) and the baptism of the Ethiopian (Acts 8:38f), but by the baptismal imagery of being buried with Christ and rising with Christ (Rom. 6:4f, Col. 2:12f). As for baptismal practice, we may listen to Calvin: 'But whether the person being baptized should be wholly immersed, and whether thrice or once, whether he should only be sprinkled with poured water—these details are of no importance, but ought to be optional to churches according to the diversity of countries. Yet the word "baptize" means to immerse, and it is clear that the rite of immersion was observed in the ancient church.'

"What matters is that water be applied visibly and generously (30.218). What matters is that the water of baptism be the Word made visible so that the rich meanings of the water of baptism as embodying God's salvation events be evident. Pouring and sprinkling—but not 'dabbing'!"

15. The issues raised by these concerns are extremely complex and involve the whole church of Christ. They have to do with the nature of God and the functional and personal character of God.

Moreover, any change in the baptismal formula will have to be by agreement of the whole church; otherwise the oneness and validity of baptism is lost. In this regard, Catherine G. González (Professor of Church History at Columbia Theological Seminary, Decatur, Georgia) summarizes the issues when she states, "The language of the original formula is clearly a problem for many, but care needs to be taken to understand what was at stake originally. In the same way that a human child shares the same humanity as the parents, so, too, the One who became incarnate as Jesus of Nazareth is completely God. Separate beings were not meant: common divinity was.

Parent and offspring would be non-gender-specific renderings. What is essential is the imagery of 'begotten,' which shows the relationship of the two. No subordination is intended by the wording. Furthermore, the entirety of the Godhead is involved in creation and redemption, and any attempt to picture the First Person as a demanding Judge in contrast to the Second Person who is a loving Redeemer does violence to the unity of God's work with us. Yet distinctions are also necessary, particularly that it is the Second Person only who became incarnate." ("Suggestions for Church Planning: Trinity Sunday" in *The Presbyterian Planning Calendar 1984–85*.)

A recent issue of *Reformed Liturgy and Music* on "Language About God," vol. 17, no. 4 (Fall 1983), deals with the concern of the language of the Trinity. In this issue of the journal, women and men write from various perspectives on the subject. See also Laurence Hull Stookey, *Baptism: Christ's Act in the Church* (the appendix, pp. 198–200, is very helpful on this issue); Dorothy L. Sayers, *The Mind of the Maker* (Harcourt, Brace & Company, 1941; chapter III deals particularly with the Trinity); and William G. Rusch, *The Trinitarian Controversy* (Fortress Press, 1980; the introduction is a very helpful, brief summary of the issues).

16. Proposed Chapter, 30.219, and the comments of John F. Jansen on pp. 27–28.

17. Chrism is olive oil in which another fragrant oil, such as balsam, is often mixed. In traditions where chrism has been used it is blessed in a prescribed liturgical ceremony.

18. The way this separation resulted is summarized on pages 18–19.

19. Daniels, op. cit., p. 87.

20. The sign of the cross is a sign of God's ownership and of engagement in the service of Christ. The earliest descriptions of Christian baptism, dating from the second century, state that the cross was traced upon the forehead of those being baptized. Second-century Christian writers tell us that this sign, used initially in baptism, was repeated often in the Christian's life. In tracing a small cross on the forehead, Christians reminded themselves of their identity as Christians. For further description of the origin and significance of the sign of the cross, see Daniels, op. cit., pp. 87, 88.

21. Oil prepared for anointing, and vessels crafted for its use, may be secured from some church supply houses, such as Fortress Church Supply Stores. Exceptionally fine concentrated oils are available from Maria G. Arctander, 6665 Valley View Boulevard, Las Vegas, NV 89118. The concentrated oil is then mixed with a high-grade food-quality olive oil for anointing. If such oil is not purchased, olive oil (or if it is not available another vegetable oil) may be used and perfume added. A small cruet or bowl facilitates the use of the oil.

22. Proposed Chapter, 30.220.

23. Great Prayer of Thanksgiving A in *The Service for the Lord's Day: Supplemental Liturgical Resource 1* (Westminster Press, 1984), liturgical text no. 183, provides a baptism variation in the opening paragraph. Great Prayer of Thanksgiving E, liturgical text no. 187, in the same resource, is particularly appropriate for use when a baptism has occurred, because its language reflects that of the baptismal liturgy.

24. The need for providing all three liturgical centers is underscored in the

Proposed Chapter: "The setting for worship should provide visible expression to the relationship between Word and Sacraments and should include a font or pool for baptism, a table for celebrating the Lord's Supper, and a pulpit or lectern for reading and interpreting Scripture" (30.212).

25. John F. Jansen in Proposed Chapter, p. 22.

26. For further elaboration on the architectural implications of baptism, see Harold M. Daniels, "Pulpit, Font, and Table," and E. A. Sovik, *Architecture for Worship* (Augsburg Publishing House, 1973), pp. 93–96. Some of the spaces for baptism depicted in Donald J. Bruggink and Carl H. Droppers, *When Faith Takes Form* (Wm. B. Eerdmans Publishing Co., 1971) reflect theological considerations. A fascinating study of the history of the way the church has provided space for baptism throughout history is John G. Davies, *The Architectural Setting of Baptism.*

27. John F. Jansen in his commentary (pp. 27–28), when noting that the Proposed Chapter does not forbid other baptismal actions as other directories of the past have done, reminds us that we have a precedent for moving beyond the purging reactions of the Reformers. Liturgical practices have been incorporated into our worship in this century which the Reformers firmly opposed. For example, Calvin abandoned the Christian year and lectionary; Puritanism and the seventeenth-century *Westminster Directory* took us further. In this century Protestants have come far in restoring the Christian year and lectionary.

Jansen also reminds us that the Reformers "had less acquaintance with the liturgical documents of the early church than we now have. For example, two early church orders prescribing the administration of baptism were not available to Calvin; the *Didache*, our earliest post-canonical directory, was not known until 1883, and the text of Hippolytus' *Apostolic Tradition* was regarded as lost until early in our century." He also notes that where there is a ceremonial vacuum, empty ceremonies are inevitably introduced, when he writes that "in abandoning some of the baptismal acts that have meant much to the ecumenical church through the centuries, sometimes we substituted other baptismal acts that have led to sheer sentimentality—like dabbing a bit of water with a rose or carnation, or supposing that water from Galilee or Jordan (usually in very diluted form) gives baptism greater meaning."

28. Proposed Chapter 30.219.

29. The paschal candle has a cross inscribed upon it with the numerals of the current year and the Greek letters alpha and omega. The candle is therefore a sign of Christ, who is present with his people from the beginning to the end. Paschal candles may be purchased from church supply houses. Directions for making a paschal candle are included in Gabe Huck, *The Three Days: Parish Prayer in the Paschal Triduum* (Liturgy Training Publications [155 Superior St., Chicago, IL 60611], 1981), pp. 113–118.

30. Proposed Chapter 30.203–204: "God's faithfulness to us signified in baptism is constant and sure, even when our faithfulness to God is not. Baptism is received only once. The efficiency of baptism is not tied to the moment when it is administered, for baptism signifies the beginning of the life in Christ, not its completion. God's grace works steadily within us, calling us to repentance and newness of life. God's faithfulness to us needs no renewal. Our faithfulness to God needs repeated renewal. Both for those

whose baptism attends their profession of faith and for those who are nurtured from childhood within the family of faith, baptism calls for decision at every subsequent stage of life's way.

"Although we receive baptism only once, there are many times in worship (including the celebration of another's baptism, the experience of the sustaining nurture of the Lord's Supper, and occasions for the renewal of our baptismal vows) when we acknowledge the grace of God continually at work in and among us, confess our ongoing need of that grace, and pledge anew our obedience to God's covenant in Christ."

31. Ibid., 30.209.

SOURCES OF THE LITURGICAL TEXTS

All scripture quotations are from the *Revised Standard Version of the Bible*, except as noted. The following quotations are altered: Deut. 7:9 (p. 82); Micah 6:8 (p. 82); Matt. 5:14–16 (p. 74); Matt. 16:26 (p. 87); John 3:3, 5 (p. 41); John 8:12 (pp. 41, 86); John 15:15–16 (p. 87); Eph. 2:10 (p. 74); Eph. 5:8, 10 (p. 82); Phil. 2:13 (p. 87); Phil. 4:7 (p. 91); Col. 3:17 (p. 87); 1 Peter 2:9 (pp. 26, 43, 74); 1 John 3:1 (p. 41).

Col. 2:12 (p. 41) is from *The New English Bible* and is altered.

Matt. 7:7; Luke 11:9 (p. 40) is from *The Bible in Today's English Version*.

Ps. 100:2–3, 5 (p. 87) is based upon various English translations of Psalm 100.

1 Peter 1:3–5 (p. 42) is adapted from the *Revised Standard Version of the Bible*, *The New English Bible*, and *The Bible in Today's English Version*.

The Apostles' Creed (pp. 28–29, 75–76, 79, 83–84, 89) is the agreed ecumenical text prepared by the International Consultation on English Texts.

The opening dialogue to the Thanksgiving Over the Water (pp. 29, 35) is derived from the opening dialogue of the Great Prayer of Thanksgiving of the Eucharist. It is an agreed ecumenical text prepared by the International Consultation on English Texts, with one slight alteration. In the last line the Consultation's text reads: "give him thanks." The text in this resource reads: "give our thanks."

The prayer beginning "O Lord, uphold . . ." (pp. 31, 76–77, 80–81, 85, 90) is based upon Isa. 11:2.

The prayer beginning "Defend, O Lord . . ." (pp. 39, 77, 81, 85, 93, 95) is based upon a prayer in *The Book of Common Worship* order for the baptism of adults. Dating from the 1552 *Book of Common Prayer*, it is an abbreviated form of a prayer accompanying the laying on of hands in various sixteenth-century German confirmation orders. It continues to be included in *The Book of Common Prayer*.

The questions and answers for alternate affirmation text D (p. 34) are based upon those in *The Worshipbook*.

FOR FURTHER READING

With few exceptions, the books in this list were in print at the time of the publication of this resource, and many may be ordered from the sources below. Out-of-print books are listed only because of their merit. They may be borrowed from a good seminary library.

CS: Curriculum Services, P.O. Box 868, William Penn Annex, Philadelphia, PA 19105; (215) 928-2700; Toll-Free–outside PA: 1-800-22PCUSA, PA outside Phila.: 1-800-52PCUSA

CSC: Cokesbury Service Centers. Toll-Free 1-800-672-1789
1661 North Northwest Highway, Park Ridge, IL 60068; (312) 299-4411
1635 Adrian Road, Burlingame, CA 94010; (415) 692-3562
201 Eighth Avenue South, P.O. Box 801, Nashville, TN 37202; (615) 749-6113

MDS: Materials Distribution Service, Presbyterian Publishing House, 341 Ponce de Leon Avenue NE, Atlanta, GA 30365; (404) 873-1549; Toll-Free–outside GA: 1-800-554-4694, GA outside Atlanta: 1-800-822-1917

OW: Office of Worship, 1044 Alta Vista Road, Louisville, KY 40205; (502) 895-2441

WCC: World Council of Churches, Interchurch Center 1062, 475 Riverside Drive, New York, NY 10115; (212) 870-2529

Baillie, Donald M. *The Theology of the Sacraments and Other Papers.* London: Faber and Faber, 1957.
This series of lectures by the late Professor of Systematic Theology in the University of St. Andrews was delivered at San Francisco Theological Seminary in 1952. It is a clear statement of sacramental theology from the Reformed perspective.

Baptism, Eucharist, and Ministry. Faith and Order Paper No. 111. Geneva World Council of Churches, 1982.
  This "convergence statement" on baptism, Eucharist, and ministry is the result of a fifty-year study process beginning with the first Faith and Order conference in 1927. Theologians from a wide spectrum of church traditions, including some not represented in the World Council of Churches, have been involved in the process. See other volumes in this bibliography related to this paper. (WWC)

Beasley-Murray, G. R. *Baptism in the New Testament.* Wm. B. Eerdmans Publishing Co., 1973.
  This is an important biblical study on baptism written by an English Baptist New Testament scholar. (CSC, MDS)

Brand, Eugene L. *Baptism: A Pastoral Perspective.* Augsburg Publishing House, 1975.
  This book, written by a Lutheran liturgical scholar, reflects the contemporary consensus about baptismal theology and practice and is recommended for adult study groups. (CSC, MDS)

Bromiley, Geoffrey W. *Children of Promise: The Case for Baptizing Infants.* Wm. B. Eerdmans Publishing Co., 1979.
  Professor of Church History and Historical Theology at Fuller Theological Seminary, Bromiley presents the case for baptizing infants from the traditional Reformed perspective. (CSC, MDS)

Burkhart, John E. "Have All the Seas Gone Dry?" *Reformed Liturgy and Music,* vol. 15, no. 4 (Fall 1981), pp. 172–177.
  Professor of Systematic Theology at McCormick Theological Seminary, Burkhart calls for a unity of word and action in baptismal liturgies, and specifically for a recovery of the central place and use of water in baptism. This article is included in a special issue of *Reformed Liturgy and Music* with the theme of baptism (see below). (OW)

Commission on Worship of the Consultation on Church Union. *An Order for the Celebration of Holy Baptism with Commentary.* Cincinnati: Forward Movement Publications, 1973.
  This baptismal rite (with commentary) was prepared for use and study by the churches participating in the Consultation on Church Union. Order from Forward Movement Publications, 412 Sycamore Street, Cincinnati, OH 45202.

Cullmann, Oscar. *Baptism in the New Testament.* Westminster Press, 1950.
  New Testament and early church history scholar Oscar Cullmann unfolds the meanings of baptism contained in the New Testament and presents the biblical basis for infant and adult baptism. (CSC, MDS)

Daniels, Harold M. "Baptism" in Harold M. Daniels, ed., *Worship in the Community of Faith.* Louisville, KY: Joint Office of Worship, 1982, pp. 45–95.

The meaning of baptism, contemporary issues related to baptism, and suggestions for baptismal practice are presented from the Reformed perspective in this study book for pastors, sessions, worship committees, and adult groups. Reflection and action suggestions are included to facilitate group study. (OW, MDS)

_____. "Pulpit, Font, and Table." *Reformed Liturgy and Music*, vol. 16, no. 2 (Spring 1982), pp. 63–72.
The spatial needs for baptism are outlined in this article on liturgical architecture. Location, shape, size, visibility, accessibility, lighting, and design are among the considerations treated. The article is included in a special issue of *Reformed Liturgy and Music* with the theme "Liturgical Space." (OW)

Davies, John G. *The Architectural Setting of Baptism*. London: Barrie and Rockliff, 1962.
A fascinating study of the history of baptismal practice and the way the church has provided space for baptism throughout Christian history. The story is traced from the earliest centuries into modern times.

Fisher, John D. C. *Christian Initiation: The Reformation Period; Some Early Reformed Rites of Baptism and Confirmation and Other Contemporary Documents*. Alcuin Club Collections No. 51. London: SPCK, 1970.
This book includes the texts of the Anglican, Reformed, and Lutheran baptismal rites and other writings on baptism dating from the sixteenth century. Brief essays introduce the documents.

Jansen, John F. "Baptism in the New Testament—Some Perspectives." *Reformed Liturgy and Music*, vol. 15, no. 4 (Fall 1981), pp. 164–171.
New Testament scholar John Jansen presents the biblical basis for baptism by describing ten different New Testament images of baptism. (OW)

Jenson, Robert W. *Visible Words: The Interpretation and Practice of Christian Sacraments*. Fortress Press, 1978.
Professor of Systematic Theology at Lutheran Theological Seminary in Gettysburg, Pennsylvania, Robert Jenson unfolds the meaning of baptism in this helpful book on the sacraments. The history of baptism is summarized and some liturgical proposals made. The relationship of baptism with penance (forgiveness of sin) and ordination is described. (CSC, MDS)

Jones, Cheslyn, Geoffrey Wainwright, and Edward Yarnold, eds. *The Study of Liturgy*. New York: Oxford University Press, 1978.
Baptismal history, theology, and practice are summarized (pp. 79–146) in this volume of liturgical studies. Essays cover the entire time from the New Testament period through a review of modern rites. Eastern as well as Western rites (Catholic and Protestant) are covered. (CSC, MDS)

Kavanagh, Aidan. *The Shape of Baptism: The Rite of Christian Initiation.* Studies in the Reformed Rites of the Catholic Church, vol. 1. Pueblo Publishing Co., 1978.

> Post–Vatican II Roman Catholic reforms in the Christian initiation of adults are given solid support in this study on the history and reform of baptismal practice written by a Roman Catholic liturgical scholar. (CSC)

Lazareth, William H. *Growing Together in Baptism, Eucharist, and Ministry: A Study Guide.* Faith and Order Paper No. 114. Geneva: World Council of Churches, 1982.

> This study guide was prepared for use with *Baptism, Eucharist, and Ministry* listed earlier. (WWC, MDS)

McNeill, John T., ed. *Calvin: Institutes of the Christian Religion.* 2 vols. The Library of Christian Classics. Westminster Press, 1960.

> Calvin's teaching on baptism may be found in Book IV, chs. 15–16 (vol. 2, pp. 1303–1359). (CSC, MDS)

Marty, Martin E. *Baptism.* Fortress Press, 1962.

> Written in a popular style by a well-known Lutheran, this book describes what God gives in baptism. Recommended for lay study groups. (CSC, MDS)

Reformed Liturgy and Music

> A quarterly journal of the Office of Worship, on worship and music from the perspective of the Reformed tradition. It regularly includes articles on a variety of subjects by leaders in the field of worship. Regular columns, book reviews, and music reviews keep readers informed about resources and events and provide guidance to pastors, musicians, and worship committees. The journal regularly provides information about the development of the series of supplemental liturgical resources, of which this volume is the second. Articles on the subject of each supplemental resource are planned in relation to the publication of each resource. The Fall 1985 issue will be particularly useful in relation to *Holy Baptism and Services for the Renewal of Baptism.* (OW)

_____, vol. 15, no. 4 (Fall 1981).

> This special issue of *Reformed Liturgy and Music* has baptism as its theme and contains the articles by John F. Jansen and John E. Burkhart referred to above, as well as "Salt and Light" (Joseph D. Small III) and "Recent Liturgies of Christian Initiation: An Ecumenical Survey" (Laurence Hull Stookey). (OW)

Schmeiser, James, ed. *Initiation Theology.* Toronto: Anglican Book Centre, 1978.

> This volume is a collection of the addresses given by major liturgical scholars at the Fourth Symposium of the Canadian Liturgical Society, "Worship '77": "Life-cycle Events and Civil Ritual" (Aidan Kavanagh);

"The New Testament" (G. R. Beasley-Murray); "The Eastern Church" (Alexander Schmemann); "The Western Church" (Leonel Mitchell); "Pastoral Considerations" (Eugene L. Brand). It is an excellent brief summary of recent developments in baptismal theology and practice. Order from the Anglican Book Centre, 600 Jarvis Street, Toronto, Ontario, Canada M4Y 2J6.

Schmemann, Alexander. *For the Life of tne World: Sacraments and Orthodoxy.* Crestwood, NY: St. Vladimir's Seminary Press, 1973.
The cosmic dimensions of the Orthodox understanding of baptism are portrayed in this brief book on the Christian approach to the world and human life from the Orthodox perspective. Appendix 2, "Sacrament and Symbol," is particularly helpful for understanding the Orthodox approach to the sacraments. Order from St. Vladimir's Seminary Press, 575 Scarsdale Road, Crestwood, NY 10707.

_____. *Of Water and the Spirit: A Liturgical Study of Baptism.* Crestwood, NY: St. Vladimir's Seminary Press, 1974.
The meaning that baptism should have in our lives is underscored in this description of baptismal belief and practice in the Eastern Orthodox tradition. Order from St. Vladimir's Seminary Press, 575 Scarsdale Road, Crestwood, NY 10707.

Searle, Mark. *Christening: The Making of Christians.* Liturgical Press, 1980.
A study of reforms in baptismal practice since Vatican II in the Roman Catholic Church written by a Catholic liturgical scholar. The focus is primarily upon the baptism of infants. (CSC)

Stookey, Laurence Hull. *Baptism: Christ's Act in the Church.* Abingdon Press, 1982.
The meaning, history, and practice of baptism are examined in this readable book by the Professor of Preaching and Worship at Wesley Theological Seminary in Washington, D.C. The author proposes reforms aimed at restoring baptism to the center of the church's life. (CSC, MDS)

Thurian, Max. *Ecumenical Perspectives on Baptism, Eucharist, and Ministry.* Faith and Order Paper No. 116. Geneva: World Council of Churches, 1983.
This volume of scholarly theological essays addresses the texts contained in the World Council of Churches Faith and Order Paper No. 111: *Baptism, Eucharist, and Ministry.* The essays were prepared by scholars who were involved in the process leading to the consensus texts. They analyze the texts from the perspective of the different traditions. (WCC)

_____ and Geoffrey Wainwright. *Baptism and Eucharist: Ecumenical Convergence in Celebration.* Geneva: World Council of Churches, 1983; and Wm. B. Eerdmans Publishing Co., 1984.
Section I of this volume is an excellent sourcebook of baptismal liturgies presently in use drawn from a wide variety of Christian traditions. The liturgies illustrate both the convergence and diversity in baptismal cele-

bration. Brief essays introduce each liturgy. Also included is a portion of the Apostolic Tradition of Hippolytus, the oldest existing document (circa A.D. 215) describing baptismal practice in the ancient church. (WCC, CSC, MDS)

Whitaker, Edward C. *Documents of the Baptismal Liturgy*, 2d ed. London: SPCK, 1970.
This book is valuable as a source in English of the most important liturgical documents on baptism from the first nine centuries of Christian history, both East and West. Each document includes a brief introduction.

White, James F. *Introduction to Christian Worship*. Abingdon Press, 1980.
Chapters V, "The Acted Sign" (pp. 145–170), and VI, "Initiation and Reconciliation" (pp. 171–202), provide a basic introduction to sacramental theology and to the meaning, history, and practice of baptism. (CSC, MDS)

_____. *Sacraments as God's Self-Giving: Sacramental Practice and Faith.* Abingdon Press, 1983.
A well-known liturgical scholar provides in this book a summary of sacramental belief and practice from an ecumenical perspective and proposes specific reforms for sacramental practice. (CSC, MDS)

Willimon, William H. *Remember Who You Are: Baptism, a Model for Christian Life*. The Upper Room, 1980.
This brief book, written in a clear, lively style, explores the meaning of baptism and its significance for our lives. An educational guide is included to facilitate its use in a church school class or adult study group. (CSC, MDS)

Yarnold, Edward. *The Awe-Inspiring Rites of Initiation: Baptismal Homilies of the Fourth Century*. London: St. Paul Publications, 1972.
Early church writings, lectures, and homilies on baptism may be foun ˙ in this volume.